AMERICA
THE BEAUTIFUL

AMERICA
THE BEAUTIFUL

Brompton

Published in 1991 by
Tormont Publications Inc.
338 St. Antoine St. East
Montreal, Canada H2Y 1A3

ISBN 0-86124-411-7

Printed in Hong Kong

Reprinted 1992

Page 1: A farm nestles in the Vermont countryside in autumn.

Previous spread: Rolling dunes create a surreal impression in California's Death Valley.

This spread: A farm in Pennsylvania near Lititz in Lancaster County — the heart of the famous Pennsylvania Dutch country.

Contents

Mount Shasta rises 14,162 feet above sea level in
the Klamath National Forest in California.

Introduction

The United States of America — a beautiful land. The fourth largest country in the world both in size and population, America stretches the full width of the North American continent from the Atlantic to the Pacific, and also includes Alaska on the edge of the Arctic and Hawaii in the tropical Pacific.

From the warm beaches of Florida to the frozen Northlands of Alaska, from the Midwest prairies to the torrid deserts of the Southwest and the snow-capped mountains of the West, America is as varied as it is vast. America is the home of the spectacular Grand Canyon, the mighty Mississippi, the thundering Niagara Falls. Unbelievably rich in resources, this huge and beautiful country harbors some of the best farming areas on the globe in its vast stretches of fertile soil. Water is plentiful in most regions, and equally precious is America's great treasure trove of minerals such as coal, copper, iron, natural gas and oil.

Only about 300 years ago, most of what is now the United States was largely a wilderness. Europeans saw in this rich and spacious land an opportunity to build new and better lives, so they arrived, thousands upon thousands, from many countries. They brought with them a vast array of skills and ideas, contributing to America's colorful cultural heritage. And they brought the ideals of freedom and liberty, setting up a government designed to protect the liberty of all. They wrote a Constitution guaranteeing freedom of speech, freedom of religion, freedom of political belief and freedom of the press — a document like none other in the world. Out of diversity came unity.

The great size and wealth of the land has challenged every generation of Americans since the first colonists. Armed with freedom of thought and action, Americans embraced that challenge. When mountains blocked the way westward, roads and railroads were built around them, through them, or over them. When floods threatened farms and cities, dams and levees were built to hold back the water. Where rainfall was scanty, great irrigation systems were built to help grow crops.

America is still changing and expanding. The cities continue to grow upward and outward. Factories turn out the greatest abundance of goods in the world. The farms are the most productive on earth.

America—a beautiful land, a fertile land, a mighty land, a happy land.

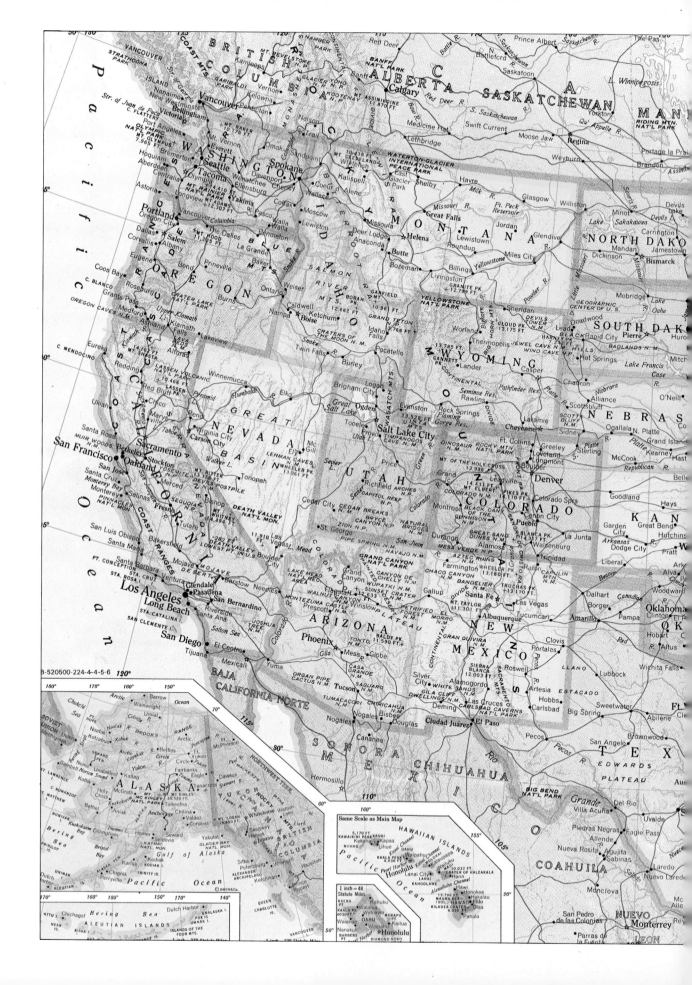

The leaves are beginning to change to their
autumn color in Peacham, Vermont.

New England

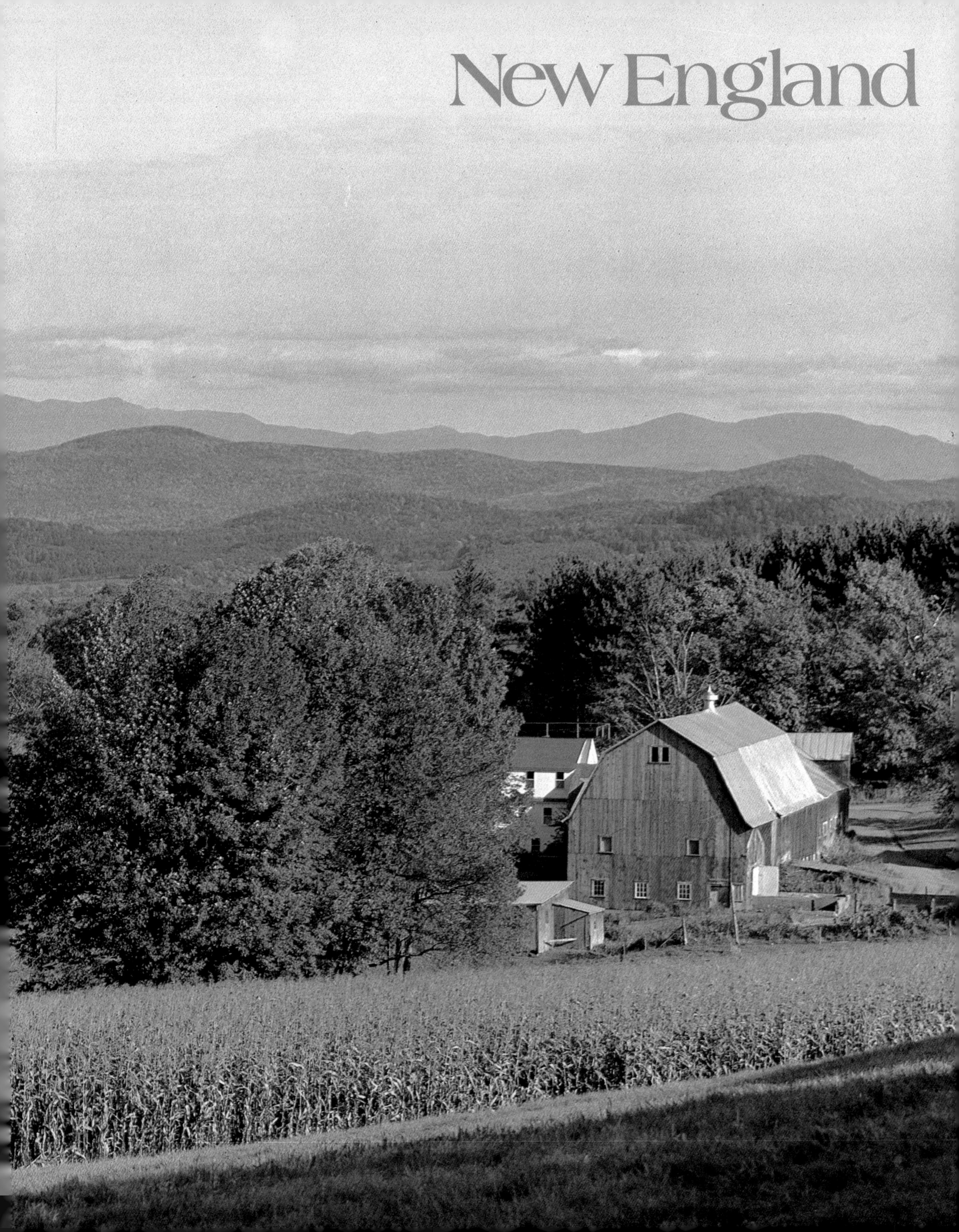

Fishing boats at Rockport Harbor, Massachusetts.
Rockport was settled in 1690 and has become, in
addition to being a fishing village, an artists'
colony. It is located at the tip of Cape Ann, north
of Gloucester.

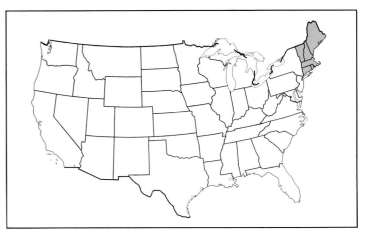

NEW ENGLAND

In the extreme northeast corner of the United States, six of the oldest states form the most homogeneous and clearly defined region in the whole country—Maine, New Hampshire, Vermont, Massachusetts, Rhode Island and Connecticut. Four were among the original 13 colonies and the other two were among the first new states in the Union.

Originally populated by Indians of the Algonquian Nation, this region of rugged mountains, watered by swift-flowing mountain streams and beautiful rivers, New England, was the place where the Pilgrim Fathers and their successors built their new homes. Despite the poor farming, the fishing was excellent and the forest rich in game and timber. The rivers supplied power for sawmills and for the factories which the practical and inventive 'Yankees' (a mysterious nickname given by the Dutch) were soon running.

New England today is highly industrialized and urbanized, yet it preserves much of its old early-American flavor. Its fishing fleet still brings in enormous catches of cod, mackerel and haddock. The picturesque fishing ports are favorite haunts of artists. Lovely old villages are still distinguished by the famous New England commons or greens and the New England churches —graceful and white, surmounted sometimes by a square bell tower, sometimes by a slender spire.

No region has more landmarks of America's struggle toward nationhood. Plymouth Rock marks the place where the Pilgrims landed after making the Mayflower Compact, America's first written instrument of democratic government. Successive waves of English colonists quickly made New England the most populous part of North America. Boston became the leading city of the New World and then the chief center of social resistance to the British Crown. Faneuil Hall, the Old North Church, the battlefields of Lexington and Concord, Bunker Hill and many more preserved sites and buildings commemorate the outbreak of the Revolution.

New England contains some of the country's most beautiful scenery—the wooded slopes of the Green Mountains of Vermont, the White Mountains of New Hampshire, the Berkshires of Massachusetts and Connecticut, the forest-covered primeval wilderness of Maine, the Connecticut River, flowing from Canada to Long Island Sound.

Opposite: New England is a land of mountains and foothills, all of which seem to explode in a blaze of reds, browns and yellows during October. Tourists make their 'autumn foliage tours' at this time and the old inns and taverns are packed. This is Montgomery Center, Vermont, population 681, about ten miles from the Canadian border.

Left: One of the historical buildings at Old Sturbridge Village in Massachusetts. Located near present-day Sturbridge, it is a re-creation of a farming hamlet in Massachusetts in the early 1800s. Centered around the green are more than 40 old houses, shops and mills. Men and women in authentic Federal period dress explain the exhibits and work at crafts. The village is also a working farm, complete with crops and livestock.

Below: An early fall snow near Oxford, New Hampshire. Winter can come early in this part of New England, and it can be severe. In parts of the state the average January temperature is a mere 14 degrees, and the wind velocity at the top of Mount Washington has been clocked at 231 miles per hour, the highest on record in any state.

Overleaf: An idyllic country town tucked in the rolling hills of Vermont, ablaze with autumn colors. Vermont is today a popular retreat for frenzied urbanites eager to escape city life.

Opposite top: Standing in front of the monumental entrance to the Boston Museum of Fine Arts, which opened in 1905, is the bronze statue, 'Appeal to the Great Spirit,' created by the American sculptor, Cyrus Dallin, in 1908.

Opposite far left: Buildings typical of Boston's Back Bay line Commonwealth Avenue, the main thoroughfare of this section, built literally on filled land in the old bay during the nineteenth century.

Opposite near left: Boston's old Haymarket Square, once the site of a hay market, has for many years now been taken over by modern buildings and highways, but street merchants still sell their goods here.

Top: Restored Quincy Market with its many shops and restaurants has become a popular tourist attraction.

Right: The center section of the State House of Massachusetts was designed by Charles Bulfinch, the first professional American architect; it was erected between 1795 and 1798.

Overleaf: Boston's modern skyline reflects the setting sun as viewed from the Cambridge side of the Charles River.

Above: The cranberry bog is typical of the coastal region of southeastern Massachusetts, where half the nation's cranberry crop is grown. The cranberry vine thrives in marshy areas and sandy bogs, which are deliberately flooded to protect plants from temperature extremes or drought.

Opposite above: A pleasure boat cruises through the Cape Cod Canal. Massachusetts' numerous inlets, estuaries, bays and small rivers allow many of the inhabitants of its eastern region to maintain boats of all kinds to enjoy the summer months at sea.

Opposite below: This old house, with its cedar shingles, is typical of the fine homes found at Siasconset, on Nantucket Island, some 30 miles south of Cape Cod. Long ago an important center of whaling and maritime trade, now Nantucket is popular as a vacation retreat.

Left: The harbor of the old fishing village of Menemsha, on Martha's Vineyard. A major whaling center in the eighteenth century, the island of Martha's Vineyard is now a quiet refuge for summer visitors.

Above: Cape Cod is a great 'flexed' arm that extends off the southern coast of Massachusetts — at its narrowest, barely two miles wide, so that, as here at North Truro, the inner bay seems separated from the Atlantic Ocean by only a strip of sand. The Cape Cod National Seashore now makes much of this outer stretch of the Cape a public preserve.

Right: At Eastham, in the central part of Cape Cod, stands the old grist windmill; dating from at least late eighteenth century, it was totally restored in the 1930s.

Left: The State House of Rhode Island is built of white Georgia marble in the Early Republican style. The General Assembly first met here in 1901.

Above: The John Brown House in Providence was designed by his brother Joseph, one of four brothers who contributed much to eighteenth century Rhode Island. Built between 1786 and 1788, the house was regarded by John Quincy Adams as the most magnificent in North America.

Below: The Old Slater Mill on the Seekonk River in Pawtucket is the oldest truly successful textile mill in the country. It was built by Samuel Slater, who immigrated here in 1790 and introduced English manufacturing techniques.

Top: These people are engaging in one of the oldest and still favorite occupations of all who come to Rhode Island — digging for clams. For the best 'clamming,' people wait till the tide is out and then venture onto the flats to dig with special rakes or hoes. Both soft and hard-shell clams are taken from the shores. The hard-shell clams were called *quahogs* by the Indians.

Above: Men sort out a sizable haul of fish at dockside.

Right: This small boat rides at rest in one of the countless inlets that line the shores of Rhode Island; with its many islands, inlets and bays, Rhode Island claims some 390 miles of coastline.

Top: One of the major diversions that Rhode Island offers is fishing.

Above: Visitors and natives agree that nothing tastes quite like food and drink at one of the many dockside restaurants that line the shores of Rhode Island.

Right: Sailing and yachting are favorite diversions offered by Rhode Island. For over a century American yachtsmen defended the America's Cup in the waters off Newport.

Opposite top: A more recent attraction in Rhode Island is the sport of ballooning.

Opposite bottom: Rhode Island's shore offers many miles of fine beaches for swimming and sunbathing. People from all over southern New England flock to them in the summer.

Opposite: The capitol of Connecticut overlooks Hartford from Capitol Hill. Deisgned by the notable nineteenth-century American architect Richard Upjohn, it was erected in 1878 and replaced the more modest old State House (a work of Charles Bulfinch from 1798). This capitol is in the Gothic Revival style, although its eclecticism and exuberance take it outside any simple historical architectural style.

Above: The final glow of sunset gives way to the lights of Hartford's modern skyscrapers that now dominate the center city. The Dutch first settled here in 1633, followed in 1635 by the English, who pushed the Dutch out by 1654. Maritime commerce in the eighteenth century and industry in the nineteenth century made the city prosperous, but it is as 'The Insurance Capital of America' that Hartford is now known. Its companies began with maritime insurance in the eighteenth century, then moved into fire insurance in the nineteenth century and gained the reputation for prompt payments that secured its future.

Right: The fast-growing city of Stamford, in Fairfield County near the Connecticut-New York border, is divided by Route I-95, and is now the home of many businesses which have moved out of New York City.

Above: The fishing docks at Stonington, a quiet old town at the easternmost point of the state, right at the border with Rhode Island. Once known as 'the Nursery for Seamen,' Stonington was a center of shipbuilding, merchant and whaling fleets, and of master seamen well into the nineteenth century, when Federal funds were allotted to build a protective breakwater. After the Civil War, with the emergence of steamships, the port lost its importance. Some fishermen still put out to sea from here, but Stonington is now best known as a refuge for more urban northeasterners who prize the beauty and solitude it offers.

Right: The town of Mystic is located on the tidal outlet of the Mystic River in northeastern Connecticut. An old port for fisherman and commercial ships, it was also a center of the colonies' maritime resistance to the British in the Revolution. In the nineteenth century, great clipper ships were built here. Now Mystic is best known for the Marine Historical Museum which harbors the only surviving whaler, the *Charles W Morgan*.

Opposite: Ocean Beach Park, south of the city of New London, lies at the mouth of the Thames River and is one of the many fine beaches along Connecticut's coast. New London is the home of the Coast Guard Academy.

Above left: Snow covers a cornfield. Some of New England's most fertile land can be found in the Connecticut River Valley, which stretches all the way from Long Island Sound north through Connecticut, through western Massachusetts and to Canada, dividing Vermont and New Hampshire.

Left: A summer scene on the edge of Bridgeport, now the largest city in Connecticut. Like virtually all American states, Connecticut's original occupation was farming. Bridgeport, at the mouth of the Pequonnock River on Long Island Sound, began as a whaling port, then moved into industry by the mid-nineteenth century to become the center of early manufacturing.

Above: A dairy farm — as indicated by its silo filled with fodder for the cattle over the winter — hibernates in the cold and snow. Connecticut still supports a thriving dairy industry — now including goats as well as cows — on its gently rolling land and fertile pastures.

Far left: Marigolds, petunias and roses front a picket fence while colorful lobster buoys decorate the weathered shingles of a typical New England house in Groton Long Point, located in eastern Connecticut on Long Island Sound. Nearby Fishers Island, a couple of miles offshore is a popular resort community where boating and fishing are favorite summertime activities.

Opposite: A fine old eighteenth-century house — the Timothy Skinner House — is one of many still found in and around the historic town of Litchfield, in northwestern Connecticut.

Left: William Gillette, a popular actor early in this century, built this medieval castle in 1919 in Hadlyme.

Above: Mark Twain had this house built for himself in 1874 on the edge of Hartford. He wrote many of his finest works while living here, but debts forced him to sell it in 1891. Now restored to its original condition and full of Twain's personal memorabilia, it is open to the public as a museum.

Top left: The Buttolph-Williams House, built by David Buttolph in 1692, is one of some 150 buildings still standing in Wethersfield that pre-date the mid-nineteenth century. Wethersfield is just south of Hartford.

Top right: The parlor of the Buttolph-Williams House occupies, along with a kitchen, the ground floor. Two bedrooms are on the second floor. The house was greatly altered in the eighteenth and nineteenth centuries, but it has now been restored and furnished with authentic period pieces. With its post-and-girt construction not far removed from medieval methods, this is one of the finest seventeenth-century houses in America.

Left: Fishing on Profile Lake, New Hampshire's Lakes Region, in the southern part of the state centered around the community of Laconia, has been a favorite with visitors for generations.

Below left: Sailing on Lake Sunapee. Mount Sunapee State Park is one of 34 state parks in New Hampshire. In July and August New Hampshire's many lakes feature sailing regattas. Excursion boats leave from Sunapee Harbor all summer.

Below: Indians taught the Europeans to make maple syrup and sugar products by tapping maple trees in the spring. After the rising sap is collected in buckets, it must be carefully heated to concentrate the sweetness.

Opposite: The beautiful colors of fall foliage enliven the banks of a stream at Wildcat Mountain. Located in the Glen Ellis Falls Scenic Area and featuring the first enclosed gondola cable car in America, Wildcat is one of eight peaks in the White Mountain National Forest that tower over a mile above sea level.

Previous spread: A placid, autumnal scene on the Swift River.

Opposite: 'Aspet,' the home of artist Augustus Saint-Gaudens, is now a National Historic Site.

Top: The Franklin Pierce Homestead in Hillsboro, the childhood home of New Hampshire's only president, was built in 1804.

Above: Strawbery Banke Museum in Portsmouth, the port to which Paul Revere rode on 13 December 1774. Strawbery Banke, Portsmouth's original name, is now a restored area featuring seventeenth- and eigthteenth-century buildings and crafts.

Previous spread: Mount Washington, the highest point in the northeastern United States, is the central peak of the White Mountains. Here the world's first cog railway was built in 1869. The highest wind speed ever observed, 231 mph, was recorded here on 12 April 1934.

Above: Woods near Lyme, north of Hanover close to the Connecticut River. Lyme was an important stagecoach stop between Boston and Montreal in the early years of the nineteenth century and has several period inns and houses.

Above right: Spring blossoms in Auburn on Massabesic Lake east of Manchester, New Hampshire.

Right: An ice sculpture at the Dartmouth Winter Carnival. Dartmouth College was established four years after the first white settlers came (1769) 'for the instruction of the Youth of Indian tribes ... and others' and has since dominated the cultural life of Hanover.

Opposite: A winter scene in the village of Marlow, on the Asheulot River. Church, school, town hall and houses all in white framed by birches in the foreground and hills on the horizon offer ample illustration of the simple elegance that has drawn visitors for 200 years.

Above: The sun sets over hills west of Charlotte, into Lake Champlain. Vermont is the only New England state with neither coast nor shoreline, but vast Lake Champlain forms about half of its western border. A ferry runs from Charlotte across the lake to Essex, New York. Charlotte boasts excellent orchard country, and its Congregational church, over 100 years old, is one of the few Greek Revival structures in Vermont.

Right: Skiers make their way down a scenic slope in the Sugarbush Valley Ski Area in Warren. The Sugarbush Valley area has an elevation of more than 4000 feet. High-elevation snowmaking insures skiing from October to mid-May, and for summer enjoyment the resort offers golf, tennis and hiking.

Opposite: Five-mile-long Mount Mansfield, the highest peak in Vermont (4393 feet), has become famous for skiing and magnificent views. Stowe and its ski areas receive 120 inches or more of snow a year. The Mt Mansfield Ski Club has done much to make American skiers international competitors.

Previous spread: Illuminated by afternoon light, mountains create a warm backdrop to a chilly autumn scene in Pittsford.

Opposite: The Walter K Howe farm, near Tunbridge, backed by October foliage. In mid-September thousands of people from nearby counties gather for the century-old Tunbridge World's Fair.

Above: A Vermont dairy farm and maple-lined road represent two of Vermont's natural industries.

Left: A toadstool from the woods near Hancock, on the White River at the edge of Green Mountain National Forest.

Overleaf: An exquisite winter scene near Barre, the center of Vermont's granite industry. The largest granite quarries in the United States are found near Barre.

Previous spread: Autumn in Waits River, Vermont. Vermont's Northeast Kingdom, which includes the counties of Orleans and Essex, is the least developed.

Left: Pemaquid Point Light, one of the famous lighthouses which dot Maine's rocky coast. A Viking skeleton dressed in armor was found nearby in 1965.

Above: Maine is known for its spectacular rugged coast. This impressive rock formation is in Acadia National Park on Isle au Haut, in Maine's Penobscot Bay.

Overleaf: A house along the coast at Kennebunkport. This town on Maine's southern coast is a summer resort as well as an arts colony.

Left: Lobstermen at work. Each year Maine supplies about 18.5 million pounds of lobster to the rest of America, more than any other state.

Below left: A seagull eyes the scenery at Cape Elizabeth, one of the most awe-inspiring shorelines in Maine. Many visit here after a storm to watch the surf pound against the jumbled rock. The painter Winslow Homer lived nearby, and President Washington ordered neighboring Portland Head Light, which is visible on clear days, into commission in 1791.

Below right: A seafood festival at Bar Harbor, the largest town on Mount Desert Island. The island includes most of Acadia National Park.

Right: Lobster buoys in Bernard. Each lobster fisherman creates his own unique color code for the buoys which indicate the location of his traps, or 'pots.' Taking lobsters from another's pots is subject to severe legal penalties, and sometimes to vigilante actions, for unless a buoy breaks adrift a man's pots are always distinguishable, and the lobstering industry is based on mutual trust.

Opposite: Black Cove in New Harbor is typical of hundreds of lobstering villages to be found along the Maine coast. Almost no seacoast town is without its small fishing fleet.

Opposite: Camden, in Maine's Penobscot region, is one of the loveliest coastal resort areas to be found in Maine or anywhere else. A popular yachting center with breathtaking long-distance views of Penobscot Bay and its many islands, the town, under which the Camden River runs before cascading into the harbor, is a delightful place to wander on foot. Musicians and music lovers can take advantage of the musical programs at the outdoor Amphitheater.

Above: Camden is the preeminent port for Maine windjammer cruises. The schooners *Mattie* and *Mercantile* are available for week-long cruises, and there are boats which cruise to nearby islands for the day. On shore, the Camden Hills rise abruptly from Penobscot Bay, a unique physical feature. The 1.4-mile summit of Mount Battie provides a breathtaking panoramic view of the bay, the islands and the peninsulas beyond.

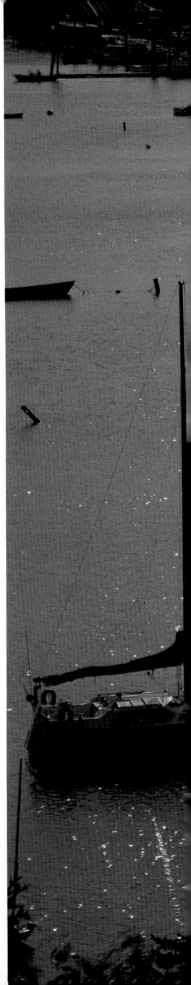

Above: Monhegan Island, nine miles out to sea, two miles long and one mile wide, has a summer population 20 times the year-round number. Most natives are lobster fishermen who take the premium-priced Monhegan lobsters from local waters from January to June.

Below: One of the many small islands — some inhabited, some uninhabited — which dot the Maine coastal waters. From earliest times Maine's many islands and rugged coast fascinated explorers. Leif Ericson landed on Monhegan in AD 1000.

Opposite: Yachting is the main attraction at Northeast Harbor, one of the coastal villages of Mount Desert Island. Summer residents and visiting yachtsmen gather by the hundreds in boats of every shape and size for regattas, races and cruises.

Above: Just north of York Beach, Maine, is Cape Neddick and the picturesque 'Nubble Light'.

Right: The surf along the rock-bound shores of Mount Desert Island in Acadia National Park, Maine. The rocky shoreline, hidden ledges and fog posed treacherous hazards for boats and ships until after the Civil War, when foghorns and lights were installed.

Below: Afternoon breakers on the Mount Desert Island coast.

Further up the Maine peninsula, but not
entirely free from the influence of bays and
inlets, is the classic village of Sheepscot.

The Middle Atlantic States

The skyline of Lower Manhattan at night.

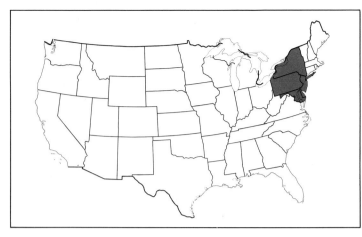

Below: Niagara Falls on the American side. In the distance is Niagara Falls, Ontario. The falls are the most-visited, most-honeymooned attractions on the North American Continent. The American Falls are 193 feet high and 1000 feet wide, and are separated from the Canadian Falls by Goat Island. From this island an elevator descends to the Cave of the Winds, where visitors put on raincoats and boots to go on a special walkway in front of the American Falls. The view is spectacular.

Opposite: The Statue of Liberty in New York Harbor; in the distance are the twin towers of the World Trade Center. The statue was given to the United States by the French people. Designed by Frederic Bartholdi, it is 152 feet high and its base on Liberty Island is about the same height. The statue itself is made of copper and the framework was designed by Gustav Eiffel, the designer of the Eiffel Tower in Paris.

THE MIDDLE ATLANTIC STATES

Along the Atlantic Coast between New England and the South lie five states—New York, New Jersey, Pennsylvania, Maryland, Delaware, plus the District of Columbia—whose total area represents only about one-thirtieth of the American land surface, but which contains nearly a fifth of the population. This busy, populous seaboard region includes the nation's largest city, New York City; its fourth largest city, Philadelphia; and five other cities with a metro area population of over one million—Washington DC, Pittsburgh, Baltimore, Newark and Buffalo.

Though the Eastern Coastal Plain is a virtually solid metropolitan belt of industrial centers and suburbs, the five states also have handsome countryside—mountains, woods, lakes and valleys. The Catskills, Poconos, Adirondacks and other Appalachian ranges offer some of the finest resort areas in the world. Side by side with the urban centers stretch miles of the world's richest farmland.

It is a region rich in history. All the states were among the original thirteen. Washington and his army spent nearly the entire Revolutionary War in this area. Philadelphia's Independence Square preserves the memories of the Declaration of Independence and the Constitutional Convention. But the most extensive historical site in the region dates from another crisis in America's history—the Civil War. The Battlefield at Gettysburg, Pennsylvania is preserved as a national military park.

Opposite top: New York's financial district as seen from the Port of Brooklyn where ships of all types and sizes may be found.

Opposite bottom: This row of buildings, now part of the South Street Seaport, was built about 1800.

Top: The old Fulton Fish Market, now incorporated into the South Street Seaport, is filled with exotic food shops and restaurants.

Left: The gambrel-roofed farmhouse at 2 White Street, built about 1780, now houses a barbershop, a typical reuse of an old building.

Above: Fresh fish were delivered right off the boats and sold daily at the Fulton Fish Market, now relocated in the Bronx.

Above: Lever House, erected in 1952, was the first of New York's glass-encased office buildings. Rising behind is the Seagram Building.
Top left: The Pierpont Morgan Library, designed by McKim, Mead and White in 1906, has a collection of early books and manuscripts.
Left: Macy's, the world's largest department store, occupies an entire block, except for the corner building with its hotdog stand.

Above: The General Assembly of the United Nations in session on the East River.
Below: The illuminated towers of the Chrysler building are typical of the dazzling New York lights.

Above: Manhattan from the East River: the UN, the Empire State and the Chrysler buildings.

Below: Paley Park, on East 53rd Street, off Fifth Avenue is a new 'pocket park.'

Above: The name says it all. The glow at the marquee of one of New York's best-known theaters explains why the street was called 'the Great White Way.'

Below: On Broadway, even the disagreeable experience of getting a parking ticket is lessened if the policeman confronting the driver is one of the many mounted officers who patrol the streets and parks.

Above: Although strictly speaking not a part of Broadway, Radio City Music Hall at Rockefeller Center seems to embody the Broadway tradition that insists 'the show must go on.' Since 1932 Radio City Music Hall has been host to about every form of theatrical production except straight plays. Once a competitor of Broadway, it is now a staunch ally in live entertainment.

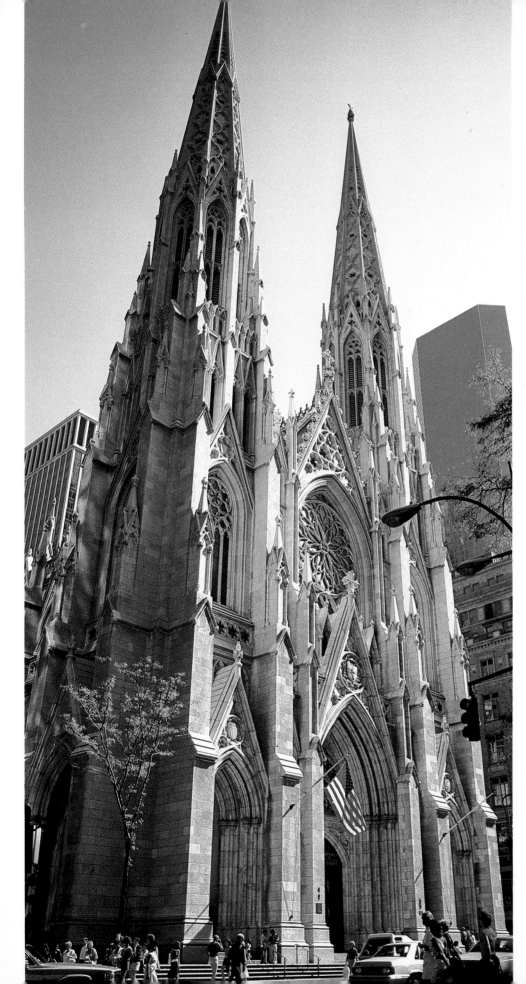

Opposite: The Trump Tower is one of the many new buildings of Fifth Avenue.
Left: St Patrick's, built on Fifth Avenue between 1858 and 1888, is the cathedral of the Roman Catholic Archdiocese of New York.
Above: 'Atlas Supporting the World' stands outside Rockefeller Center.
Below: A traditional part of the St Patrick's Day parade up Fifth Avenue is the pipe bands.

Above: A group of musicians give an *al fresco* concert on a corner of Washington Square Park. Many musicians, from classical violinists to folksingers to jazz saxophonists, can be heard on the sidewalks and parks of New York. Some play to earn money, while others, like this group, play for their own pleasure.

Opposite top: Some of 'New York's Finest' take a break. The New York Police Department, although reduced in numbers, remains the nation's largest, and women form an increasingly large percentage of the force.

Opposite far left: A New York City fireman pauses in his exertions by a firetruck. Many firemen have lost their lives in the city's service. There is a moving memorial to these brave men and women in St John the Divine.

Opposite near left: The diversity of nationalities in New York is evident on every street. Although some groups readily assimilate, others retain and display their distinct identities in custom as in dress.

Right: Two weary shoppers rest in front of the Fifth Avenue windows of B Altman's, one of Fifth Avenue's department stores. With the latest in fashion, fads and foods, and the density of its stores, the city is a favorite for New York and suburban shoppers.

Above: Ferns thrive in the forest near Ansonia, in northcentral Pennsylvania.

Right: A painted turtle suns in the Montezuma National Wildlife Refuge, northern New York.

Below: A gull wades at the Robert Moses State Park, the western tip of Fire Island, New York.

Opposite: Glen Cascade, one of the many falls of the Genesee River as it cuts through Letchworth State Park in western New York.

The Erie Canal, the first important waterway built in America and completed in 1825, winds its way through the farmlands of the Mohawk Valley in central New York.

Above: The Bear Mountain Bridge spans the Hudson River north of West Point, New York. It is a major thruway to the popular Bear Mountain State Park on the western bank and to the Pocono Mountains of Pennsylvania, just an hour away.

Right: A solitary house adds a touch of white to the green expanse of the Allegheny Mountains, as they reach into New York, just across the border from Pennsylvania.

Opposite top: A tiny marina on Otsego Lake, west central New York. Cooperstown, home of the Baseball Hall of Fame, is also on Otsego Lake, making this area very popular with tourists.

Opposite bottom: A bright red barn challenges the autumn foliage in eastern New York. New York boasts rich farmlands, excellent vineyards and many dairy farms as well as scenic beauty and wonderful summer hideaways.

The mighty Niagara Falls, in the soft sunset light.

Opposite: The Clinton Mill, in Clinton, New Jersey, was built in 1763 by David McKinney, the first settler in the area. Used to grind flaxseed, grain, talc and graphite, it operated continuously until 1920.

Above: Elegant historic homes grace the streets of charming Old Cape May, on the New Jersey shore's southernmost tip. Cape May was the first and most aristocratic seaside resort in America.

Top: Atlantic City and its famous boardwalk. The gem of the Garden State's vacation land, Atlantic City has enjoyed renewed vitality in recent years as the 'Las Vegas' of the East.

Overleaf: Many come to Atlantic City to try their luck at gambling, but many also enjoy the city's fine white sand beaches, which are ceremoniously 'unlocked' at the beginning of each summer season.

Right: A Pennsylvania farm in the Pocono Mountains. This area of old, relatively low mountains not only is fine farming country, but it is a resort area, with year-round activities, drawing swimmers, fishermen and skiers from all over the East Coast.

Opposite: Independence Hall in Philadelphia. It is a part of Independence National Historical Park, a group of Colonial buildings centered around Independence Square at Sixth and Chestnut Streets. Actually, Independence Hall is the old State House, and it was here where the Declaration of Independence and the United States Constitution were signed, and where George Washington accepted command of the Continental Armies. The capital of the United States from 1796 to 1800, Philadelphia was once the second largest city in the English-speaking world. The city was founded by William Penn in 1682 as a Quaker colony. He named his 'Greene Countrie Towne' Philadelphia, a Greek name that means 'City of Brotherly Love.'

Below: A covered bridge in Pennsylvania. There are many theories about why covered bridges were built. One theory states that they were covered to keep the sun and the rain from the bridge bed in order to slow down the rotting of the timbers. Another says that in colder regions the snow would build up faster on bridges than on the roads because of the melting effect of the dirt under the road. In any event, in winter, snow had to be shoveled onto the bridge so the sleighs could pass.

Above: An Amish family bails hay during the harvest season in Lancaster County, heart of Pennsylvania's Dutch country. Profoundly religious, the Amish have tenaciously clung to their traditions, language, and customs for over two centuries. In spite of their simple equipment, they are master farmers of their land.

Opposite: Philadelphia's Elfreth's Alley is said to be the United States' oldest continuously inhabited residential street. The narrow two-story brick houses, a few of which date back to 1725, are typical of colonial Philadelphia. Once a year, on Elfreth's Alley Day, the homes are open to the public and many visitors are surprised by some of the ultra-modern interiors.

Left: The Liberty Bell stands enshrined in its glass pavilion on the Mall north of Independence Hall. Cast in Whitechapel, London, the bell cracked during its first test run. Recast by two local foundrymen, it summoned the city folk to the first public hearing of the Declaration of Independence on 8 July 1776. The bell cracked again when it last tolled at the funeral of Chief Justice John Marshall in 1835.

Overleaf: An Amish buggy accents the peace and beauty of Pennsylvania's Dutch country.

Left: Sugar maple trees stand in a meadow in Ricketts Glen State Park in northcentral Pennsylvania, west of Wilkes-Barre. The 13,000-acre park contains the Glens Natural Area, a Registered Natural Landmark; its principal attraction is Kitchen Creek, formed by three streams originating in glacially formed lakes. The creek winds three miles through the Glens, falling about 1000 feet with 28 waterfalls — one 1000 feet high.

Above: Bright autumn leaves lie like jewels along a stream in Ricketts Glen State Park in northcentral Pennsylvania. The park's many streams and creeks have shaped the terrain over the years, their rushing waters producing ledges, potholes and flumes.

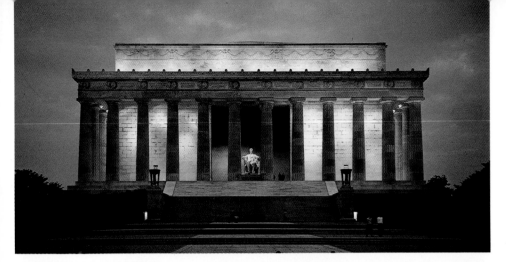

Opposite: The Washington Monument dominates the Mall in Washington DC and seems to tower over the Capitol Dome on the horizon. This obelisk is precisely 555 feet, 5 1/8 inches high, and is said to be the tallest masonry structure in the world.

Left: The Lincoln Memorial in Washington is built like a Greek temple and faces the Washington Monument across a long reflecting pool. The 19-foot statue of Lincoln by Daniel Chester French looks as though it had been carved from a single block of marble; it is actually 28 separate pieces. The Memorial was opened in 1922.

Below: Cherry blossoms in front of the Jefferson Memorial at the Tidal Basin in Washington.

Previous spread: Crowned by the American flag, the imposing White House, 1600 Pennsylvania Ave, N.W., stands resplendent on a glorious spring morning. The residence of America's First Family, it was completely restored from 1948 to 1952, and of its 132 rooms, eight are on display today. Completed in 1800, the White House has been home to every president since John Adams.

Opposite: L'Enfant, the French engineer who designed the Capitol, chose Jenkins Hill as the site for his colossal structure. The dome, cast in iron, weighs 4455 tons and rises 287 feet above the ground.

Above: The Washington Cathedral, modeled after the great Gothic cathedrals of Europe, has been under construction since 1907.

Top right: Georgetown is Washington's finest residential neighborhood. Charming brick homes of the Federal period — many of which have been transformed into chic shops and elegant restaurants offering the finest cuisines from around the world — line its cobblestone streets.

Right: The Paleontological exhibit in Washington's Museum of Natural History showcases life-size dinosaur skeletons, which have made this exhibit the most popular in the whole museum.

Opposite: Ferns and beeches form a subtle contrast in the forest near Brady's Pond in the Pocono Mountains of northeastern Pennsylvania.

Left: The salt marshes that lie along Delaware's bay shore are a winter home or stopover for migratory waterfowl; threatened by industrial and urban pollution, they have been preserved by conservationists. Not coincidentally, the landscape recalls that of Holland, and the first settlers of Delaware were the Dutch.

Below: The greenish surface of the stagnant pool contrasts with the white water of the rushing brook in Warren County, in northwestern New Jersey.

Above: The Allee House, built in 1753 by the Dutchman Abraham Allee, is located in Bombay Hook National Wildlife Refuge just north of Leipsic, Delaware. The Refuge is thrilling for birdwatchers, who can observe many species of migrating and wintering fowl on the 110 acres.

Top: Hundreds of marinas line the bays and inlets off Maryland's famed Chesapeake Bay. Sailing is a way of life for coastal Marylanders. The handsome Martha Lewis will spend the summer in the Bay, before she is sailed south to Florida for the winter months.

Right: Cattle graze on a farm in autumn in the beautiful country north of Frederick, Maryland. The center of Maryland's 'Not-So-Wild West,' Frederick is a few miles west of New Market, the 'Antiques Capital of Maryland,' where one can shop in over four dozen high-quality antique shops.

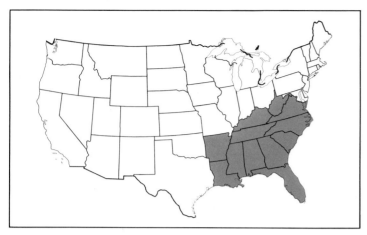

THE SOUTH

The 12 Southern States—Georgia, North Carolina, South Carolina, Kentucky, Virginia, West Virginia, Florida, Alabama, Mississippi, Louisiana, Arkansas and Tennessee—are rich in history and beauty. From the first permanent English settlement in America, founded at Jamestown in 1607, slowly grew a large and prosperous colony named Virginia, stretching west to the Mississippi River. Ultimately it was carved into three states—Virginia, West Virginia and Kentucky.

The first explorers of this vast region were Spanish. Ponce de León's exploration of both Florida coasts was followed by Hernando de Soto's 4000-mile trek into the interior, in which he penetrated the future states of Georgia, Tennessee, Alabama and Mississippi before discovering and crossing the Mississippi. In 1565 the first permanent settlement of the future United States by Europeans was accomplished by the Spaniards at St Augustine, Florida. Farther west a French settlement took root at New Orleans early in the eighteenth century. Early English settlements at Charleston, Savannah, Wilmington and elsewhere also survive.

Although the South was the earliest part of the United States to be settled by Europeans, it is only within the last few decades that its rich history, its balmy climate, its food, entertainment and hospitality have made it an important tourist area. The 12 states run the gamut from mile-high forested mountain peaks to rolling farmlands to palm-shaded subtropical beaches.

The South is the only region in the United States equally rich in historic souvenirs from the two great crisis of American history—the Revolution and the Civil War.

Right: A mill on Glade Creek in West Virginia, the state that has been described as 'the most southern of the northern, the most northern of the southern, the most western of the eastern, the most eastern of the western states.'

Previous Spread: The Orton Plantation House in North Carolina. The plantation manor house, with its tall pillars and portico in front, is an architectural reminder of the South of the past.

Above: Known locally as fishpond oaks, these trees are typically found growing as here, on the edge of a pond in the wilds of West Virginia.

Far left: This lovely waterfall is one of several that convey water down through the deep gorge of Cloudland Canyon State Park, located on the edge of Lookout Mountain in northwestern Georgia. This remote region once belonged to the Cherokee Indians; legend claims that there is a rich lead mine hidden somewhere within this territory.

Left: A section of the cypress and black gum swamp located on the floodplain of the Congaree River in central South Carolina. Visible are some so-called cypress knees — rounded growths from root systems that project above the water's surface.

Right: This delicate blossom is that of the oak leaf hydrangea, which grows on the slopes of Lookout Mountain in northeastern Alabama. Mountain laurel and rhododendron also bloom here in late spring. The Lookout Mountain extends into Georgia.

Left: The 215-foot high stone bridge near Natural Bridge, Virginia. Before the settlers came, Indians worshipped this phenomenon of nature. Thomas Jefferson bought the gorge and the bridge for 20 shillings in 1774, building a cabin for visitors and hiring caretakers to maintain the tourist attraction.

Opposite: A scene in the Blue Ridge Mountains of Virginia, overlooking the Shenandoah Valley.

Below: 'Monticello,' the mansion that Thomas Jefferson designed for himself, is one of the most beautiful estates in Virginia and is considered a classic of American architecture. Begun in 1769, it took 40 years for Jefferson to complete. It was here that he took his bride, Martha, in 1772, and it was here that he died on 4 July 1826. The house contains many of his inventions, such as dumb-waiters, hidden stairways and a clock operated by cannonball weights.

Above: The *Balmoral Castle* is one of two trains that circles Busch Gardens, a theme park featuring recreated seventeenth-century European villages near Williamsburg, Virginia.

Left: America's most celebrated home, Mount Vernon, is located fifteen miles from Washington DC in Virginia. George Washington lived there from 1754 until his death in 1799.

Opposite top: Cannons are fired in front of the Governor's Palace in Old Colonial Williamsburg, Virginia, the largest reconstructed eighteenth century village in the world. Once the capital of the British Empire in the New World and then a hotbed of revolutionary activity, Williamsburg fell into disarray until the late 1920s when its restoration began.

Opposite bottom: Replicas of the *Susan Constant,* the *Godspeed,* and the *Discovery* — the three small ships that brought the first successful English settlers to the New World in 1607 — are moored at the James River dock in Jamestown Festival Park, Jamestown, Virginia.

Above: An old mill stands dry by the roadside near Millpoint, West Virginia.

Right: Virginia has more plantation houses than any other state, and most are found between Williamsburg and Richmond. The Shirley Plantation House was the home of Robert E Lee's mother, Anne Hill Carter, and has been in the Hill Carter family since 1723. Still in the home are the original furnishings, silver and family portraits.

Opposite top: The imposing Governor's Palace in Old Colonial Williamsburg, Virginia, was completely destroyed by fire in 1781. Reconstruction began in 1931 based on archaeological excavations, a copper plate of the building, and Thomas Jefferson's 1779 floor plan. Jefferson was the second of the Commonwealth of Virginia's first two governors — Patrick Henry was the first — to hold office in the Georgian-style English manor, originally completed in 1720.

Opposite bottom: Jamestown Festival Park, just one mile outside of Jamestown, Virginia, showcases the dwellings in which the settlers first lived.

Overleaf: A thoroughbred racehorse farm in the Bluegrass region of Kentucky.

Pages 132 & 133: The delicate pink-purple blossoms of the redbud tree brighten the banks of a stream winding through the Bernheim Forest near Clermont in western Kentucky.

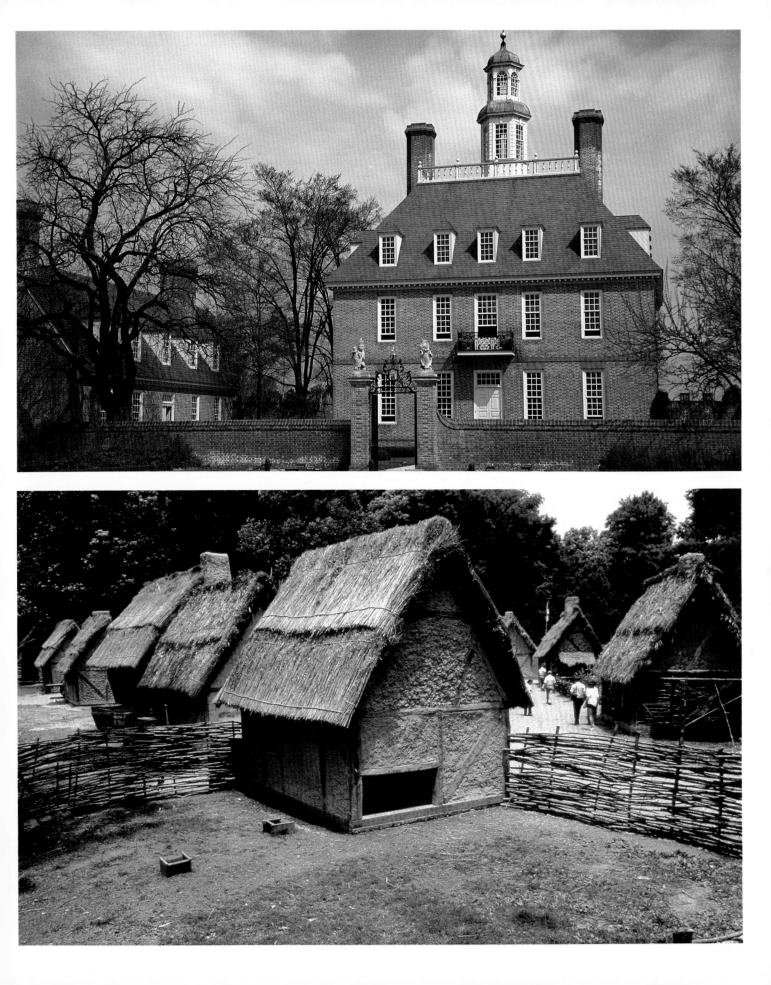

Opposite: The Biltmore House in Asheville, North Carolina, was built in the 1890s by George Vanderbilt, the grandson of the shipping and railroad tycoon, Vanderbilt 'The Commodore.' Architect Richard Morris Hunt and landscaper Frederic Law Olmsted who designed New York City's Central Park, fashioned the estate after the French chateaus of the Loire Valley.

Top: Spring House in Middleton Place, near Charleston, South Carolina. It took over 100 men and 10 years to complete Middleton Place in the mid 1700s. The estate was also the home of Henry Middleton, president of the first Continental Congress.

Above: Edisto Island, first settled in 1690, has become the most popular family vacation beach on South Carolina's southern shore. The three miles of white sand beaches are also a beachcomber's paradise; the ocean deposits there some of the coastline's finest seashells.

Overleaf: Pinks and purples bathe Manteo Beach at sunset, Roanoke Island, North Carolina.

Left: Little Pigeon Creek winds through Great Smoky Mountains National Park, which provides a protected home for a wealth of flowering plants, trees, over 200 bird species and numerous mammals.

Above: Tokawa Falls in North Carolina is one of many waterfalls in Great Smoky Mountains National Park. The park covers over 800 square miles, stretching from eastern Tennessee to western North Carolina.

Right: Cattails are caught at sunset at Lake Phelps in North Carolina, part of the Dismal Swamp National Wildlife Refuge (most of which is in Virginia). Covering some 600 square miles, with Lake Drummond at its heart, it is truly a swampy wilderness.

Overleaf: Autumn's paintbrush has begun to color the trees of the Great Smoky Mountains National Park in Tennessee and North Carolina.

Above: The King of Rock 'n' Roll, Elvis Aaron Presley, is immortalized in this statue in Memphis, Tennessee. Though not his hometown (Tupelo, Mississippi, was), it was in Memphis that the talented young man was discovered, recording his first hit *That's Alright Mama* at the Sun Studio. It was also in Memphis that Elvis died on 16 August 1977.

Top left: Memphis' famous Beale Street, on a busy morning. In Beale Street's Pee Wee Saloon W C Handy first sang the sad and lonesome melodies which made him the 'Father of the Blues.' Memphis' heritage is not only musical; the city is both the world's largest spot-cotton market and hardwood lumber center.

Left: Touches of bright orange and yellow enliven the picturesque Main Street of Jonesborough, Tennessee, in the early fall.

Opposite top: Recently converted to a hotel, Nashville's Union Station was once the grandest railroad depot in the South. Its fantastic Romanesque design closely resembles H H Richardson's famous Allegheny Courthouse in Pittsburgh.

Opposite bottom: Visitors climb the steep slopes of Lookout Mountain, 2225 feet high, to take in the spectacular view of the Tennessee River's Moccasin Bend Valley below, in which sits the famous city of Chattanooga. Because of its strategic placement, Chattanooga was first a great Cherokee trading center and then a battleground during the Civil War.

Opposite: The Twin Towers in Atlanta, the convention capital of the country, are the seat of Georgia's government. Since Jimmy Carter's presidency, Georgia has seen a 40 percent increase in tourism.

Above: Helen, a Bavarian-style village in northern Georgia's Appalachian Mountains, features charming gingerbread-trimmed buildings.

Below: The Atlanta Braves in action. In 1974 baseball superstar Hank Aaron broke Babe Ruth's home run record by hitting his 715th home run in Atlanta's Fulton County Stadium.

The tranquil beauty of Florida's Key West shines
through at sunset.

Left: Canoers in the Okefenokee Swamp in southeast Georgia, near Waycross. The Okefenokee is the largest preserved fresh-water swampland in the United States, covering 700 square miles. The early Creek Indians called it 'The Land of the Trembling Earth,' and its lakes of dark brown water, lush with moss-draped cypress trees and mysterious streams are the headwaters of the Suwannee River, about which Stephen Collins Foster waxed so eloquently.

Opposite: Miami Beach, Florida, sometimes called 'America's International Playground,' where celebrities and sunbathers are squeezed onto an island a mere eight miles long and from one to three miles wide. This is Hotel Row, where property sells for thousands of dollars per front foot. It is hard to believe that it was once a palmetto swamp, populated mostly by snakes and mosquitoes, until John S Collins failed in his attempt to grow avocados there and turned to real estate. He auctioned off the land (much of it underwater), brough sand to turn it into solid ground, and built what was then the longest wooden bridge in the United States, to connect it with Miami.

Below: The Everglades, stretching over 2100 square miles, in southern Florida, is the largest subtropical wilderness in North America. It is a spectacular area — half land, half water. Indians called it 'River of Grass.'

Above: Against a crimson backdrop, a rocket stands at Cape Canaveral's launch site. A few miles down the road on Merritt Island is the famed NASA moon-launch area from where Apollo 11 was launched 16 July 1969 to begin man's first lunar landing expedition.

Left: Cinderella's Castle, aglow in the night, towers over Fantasyland, one of Disney World's six sections. The 'Magic Kingdom' includes Main Street USA, Adventureland, Frontierland, Liberty Square and Tomorrowland. But the most popular attraction of all is the extravagant Epcot Center, inaugurated in 1982, and visited by millions yearly.

Opposite top: The television show *Flipper,* first aired in 1964, immortalized the dolphin as Florida's mascot. Marineland, south of St Augustine on the Atlantic coast, has six fabulous shows a day and is almost always sold out.

Opposite bottom: Marketing savvy led this food truck to go Art Deco. Its geometric designs and pastel colors echo the tropical Art Deco architecture of the Old Miami Beach historic district in the background. From the late 1920s through the 1930s this section of town was a stronghold of the genre, eager to display the exuberance and opulence of what Miami Beach had then become, a sun worshipper's paradise.

Overleaf: A glorious rainbow graces the tropical beauty of Captiva Island on Florida's Gulf Coast, west of Fort Myers. Marinas brighten the island's coves, while strewn on its white sand beaches are many seashell gems.

Left: Perhaps the quintessential image of Southern wilderness — cypress trees in wetland, here at Catahoula Lake, central Louisiana.

Above: The Everglades National Park at the southern tip of Florida, noted as a refuge for birds, is rich in exotic flora and fauna.

Opposite: A crimson sunset over Lake Hart in Orange County, central Florida. The web-like beauty of the swamp cypress tree is an eerie reminder of the dangerous marshes in Florida's lowlands.

Above: Shark Valley in Everglades National Park. A variety of wildlife and the rare wood stork inhabit this wide and shallow waterway which eventually empties into the Shark River.

157

Above: A common egret at the J N 'Ding' Darling National Wildlife Refuge on Sanibel Island, southern Florida — a fine birding site.

Right: Big Cypress Swamp is part of the Everglades National Park in Florida.

Below: A young alligator suns itself in the Corkscrew Swamp Sanctuary, noted for its stand of virgin bald cypresses.

Opposite: Wild Boston fern flourish in the Highland Hammock State Park in Florida.

Previous spread: In a stunning interplay of reds, oranges and pinks, the sun sets over the mighty Mississippi River which winds its way along Mississippi's western border.

Above: The Hernandez House, on St Charles Avenue in New Orleans, Louisiana, typifies the elegance and grandeur of the South's antebellum homes. A masterpiece of Second Empire architecture, the Hernandez House, with its intricate mansard roof, is one of the few of its kind remaining in New Orleans.

Far right: New Orleans' thriving Central Business District at night. Before the Civil War, this area was called the 'American Section,' in contrast to the French Quarter, because of the high numbers of Anglo-Americans who settled there after the Louisiana Purchase. Also known as the Faubourg St Marie, the area has seen phenomenal growth in the last twenty years and its twentieth-century structures sharply contrast with nineteenth-century buildings to create an exciting and charming commercial center.

Right: An antique musical instrument hangs above Dixie's Restaurant on Bourbon Street in New Orleans' French Quarter, reminding passersby of the city's musical heritage. Jazz and blues were born in New Orleans, they say, and even today music plays an important part in the city's mystique.

Left: Decatur Street in New Orleans' French Quarter, the *Vieux Carré*, or 'Old Square.'

Below: Apartment houses in the French Quarter of New Orleans show their typically intricate wrought-iron work. In this section of New Orleans every house and shop has its own special history. Many *Vieux Carré* homes turn their backs on the streets and open out into flagstoned patios shaded by palms and banana plants. In this private world, the family has breakfast, the housewife does her chores, and cool drinks are served on a summer's evening. The population is cosmopolitan with its Creoles (descendants of the original French and Spanish colonists), Cajuns (descendants of the Acadians who were driven from Nova Scotia by the British in 1755) and other groups whose ancestors came from the Caribbean and Africa.

This spread: New Orleans' exhilarating Mardi Gras begins two weeks before Mardi Gras Day or Shrove Tuesday, and over 60 parades stream through the streets of *Vieux Carré*, the city's French Quarter. Old silk-stocking carnival balls (by invitation only), street bands, masquers, parties and food orgies take over city life and fun and silliness have full reign. On Mardi Gras Day, the festivities reach their climax when over one million people in carnival garb follow the floats down St Charles Avenue, Canal Street and Bourbon Street, calling out 'Throw me somethin' Mister!' and then scrambling for the precious trinkets and doubloons thrown from the floats.

Above: The White House of the Confederacy in Montgomery, Alabama, was the lavish home of Jefferson Davis, president of the Confederacy. He took oath as president in 1861 on the steps of the Capitol across the street. Marching down Dexter Avenue to a new tune called 'Dixie,' Davis did not anticipate that Alabama, then heartbeat of the Confederacy, would be torn asunder in the Civil War.

Opposite: The residence today of the president of the University of Alabama, the Gorgas House in Tuscaloosa is a splendid example of antebellum architecture. It was named after the courageous Dr William C Gorgas who valiantly fought the yellow fever epidemic during the ill-fated construction of the Panama Canal.

Left: Intricate iron grill work, fine old mansions and sumptuous gardens are the pride of Mobile, Alabama, the Azalea Center of the state. The Bellingrath estate and gardens are the South's most famous because of the hundreds of thousands of azaleas on display and their elaborate and sophisticated landscaping. A touch of Frenchness pervades the atmophere of this charming shoretown: Mobile was Fort Conde in 1711, capital of the French Colonial Empire, before it was moved to New Orleans. Even so, Mobile retained its *savoir vivre*, lavish elegance and great charm.

The Midwest and the Plains

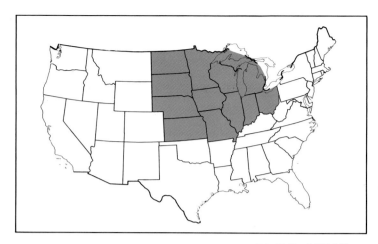

THE MIDWEST AND THE PLAINS

There are eight Midwest States—Ohio, Indiana, Illinois, Michigan, Wisconsin, Minnesota, Iowa and Missouri—and four Plains States—North Dakota, South Dakota, Nebraska and Kansas. Combined, the two sections make up a huge part of the continent and have a population of some 62 million.

The region is broad and flat, with many clusters of rolling hills. The northern stretch is studded with lakes and surviving patches of the magnificent forest the first explorers found. Early French explorers and trappers dotted the area with French names—Eau Claire, Terre Haute, Pierre, Detroit, Fond du Lac, St Louis and Vincennes, Indiana, which was the scene of George Rogers Clark's Revolutionary War victory which helped insure that part of the vast region would be a part of the new United States. The end of that war was a signal for tremendous immigration from the Eastern Seaboard. Ohio became a state in 1803, the same year that the Louisiana Purchase gave the vast trans-Mississippi area to the Union.

The first European visitors west of the Mississippi were Coronado and his men in 1541, but it was not until the journey of Marquette and Joliet in 1634 that the real penetration began. During the late seventeenth and early eighteenth centuries, French fur traders roamed Kansas and Nebraska and by 1743 entered the Dakotas, and in 1804 Lewis and Clark made their historical exploration of the Louisiana Purchase—that gigantic real estate bargain. Settlers followed and by the 1840s Kansas was a jumping-off point for covered wagon trains headed west.

Almost everything can be found in the region, except salt water. Huge cities and small towns, major coal, oil and gas deposits, iron ore ranges, diversified factories, magnificent wheat and corn fields, acres of oats, rye, flaxseed, soybeans, sugar beets, fruit, livestock and dairies.

Previous spread: A farm in the south central part of Wisconsin. Much of the area contains rolling hills that are the result of glacial moraines—extremely fertile formations.

Right: A Kansas wheat field. In 1981 Kansas produced 305 million bushels of this crop, second only to North Dakota. Kansas's total was almost 12 percent of all the wheat grown in the United States that year.

Left: Downtown Chicago at night. This huge city on the shores of Lake Michigan is the chief metropolis of the center of the country. The lakeshore is the city's showcase, with a superb chain of parks and parkways flanking the shore, and the city's tallest and finest buildings rising behind them. Chicago was the birthplace of the modern skyscraper and contains many notable examples of modern architecture and engineering, including the imposing Standard Oil Building in the center, which rises to a height of 1454 feet, making it the tallest building in the world. To the right of it, with the two poles on top, is the John Hancock Center—1127 feet tall.

Below: One of the most beautiful landmarks in Chicago is Buckingham Fountain in Grant Park. Also in the park, which is located between Lake Michigan and the heart of the city, are the John G Shedd Aquarium, the Adler Planetarium and the distinguished Art Institute of Chicago.

Previous spread: Looking north along Chicago's Michigan Boulevard, one can see a startling panorama of giant buildings such as the Wrigley Building (with the clock tower), and the Tribune Tower (Gothic building across the street).

Top left: The world-famous clock of Marshall Field's department store on State Street, with the Chicago Theater's marquee as a backdrop.

Top right: A vendor at Wrigley Field, home of the Chicago Cubs, the 1984 National League East Champions.

Above: Spinnakers strain in the wind as eager contestants set off in the Chicago to Mackinac race, held annually in June.

Opposite: Chicago's wide streets stretch for miles, and the city planners have not forgotten to include refreshing spots of greenery.

Left: Garden of the Gods area in Shawnee National Forest, Illinois.

Above: Pictured Rocks National Lakeshore near Munising, Michigan.

Overleaf: Mann's Chapel, near Rossville, Illinois, was erected in 1857, east of the Old Hubbard Trail to Chicago. Restored in 1959 for Rossville's centennial celebration, the original church bell still tolls today for the one or two weddings a year held there.

Above: The Straits of Mackinac join Lake Huron and Lake Michigan. Soaring over the wide channel is the third longest suspension bridge in North America—the Mackinac Bridge. This point is the only place in America where the sun rises on one Great Lake (Huron) and sets on another (Michigan). Mackinaw City began as a French trading post and became Fort Michilimackinac about 1715. It was taken over by the British in 1761 and two years later was captured by Indians. St Ignace was founded over three hundred years ago by the French priest-explorer, Father Marquette. It is also the gateway to Michigan's splendidly beautiful Upper Peninsula with its striking scenery.

Opposite: Holland, Michigan has the largest concentration of people of Dutch descent in America. Each May, its Tulip Festival draws thousands of visitors to see thousands of acres of blooming tulips and to watch Dutch ceremonies, which include street scrubbing, clog dancing and parades in native costumes.

Left: A view of Mackinac Island, Michigan, in the Straits of Mackinac, the most famous of the hundreds of islands in Michigan, sometimes called 'The Bermuda of the North.' Held by the French until 1760, it became English after Wolfe's victory at Québec, was turned over to the US at the end of the Revolution, was British during the War of 1812, and then reverted.

Above: A law student relaxes in the stunning setting of the University of Michigan's Law Quadrangle. The Tudor and Gothic architecture recalls the universities of Oxford and Cambridge in England, after which architects York and Singer of New York fashioned the Law School. The University of Michigan, in Ann Arbor, is known not only for its high academic standards but also for the beauty of its campus.

Top left: Students head across campus in the brisk Michigan winter, passing under the Engineering Arch. Professor Charles Dennison designed the Arch in 1904 to maintain the traditional walkway through campus.

Left: The University of Michigan Stadium, completed in 1927 and renovated in 1976, is the largest collegiate football stadium in the nation.

Opposite top: The General Motors World Headquarters building in Detroit, Michigan, showcases special exhibits of GM's latest products. Located in Detroit's New Center area, the building is part of a renaissance effort by officials to bring new life to the city.

Opposite bottom: The Queen of the Shiawassee is an authentic paddleboat, which presides over the Chesaning Showboat Festival, Chesaning's annual July bash in Michigan.

Overleaf: Autumn trees brighten the countryside near Good Hart, Michigan.

Left: Made of square hewn logs, the Newcom Tavern is the oldest standing building in Dayton, Ohio. Built in 1796 for Colonel George Newcom, the tavern served as church, courthouse, and schoolhouse, as well as the Colonel's residence, for the original settlers to the area. In 1896, at Dayton's centennial, the tavern became the town's first museum. Moved to Carillon Park in 1964 from Dayton's downtown, it is the hub of the city's first historic park.

Top: The beautiful Victorian Romanesque interior of the Old Arcade in Cleveland, Ohio. The first skylighted mall in the nation, the Old Arcade stands five stories high and was completed in 1890. The intricate ironwork was commissioned by Van Dorn Ironworks, whose previous area of expertise was jail cells.

Above: A brilliant rainbow reaches up into an ominous sky, sitting low above a farmstead in Ohio's countryside.

191

Right: Indiana has its covered bridges, too. This one is now used merely for walking. It dates back to 1876 and is located in Parke County, near Rockville.

Opposite: Looking across the Mississippi River toward St Louis, the most striking thing that one sees is the mammoth Gateway Arch, symbolizing the city's nickname of 'The Gateway to the West.' An architectural marvel that soars to 630 feet, the stainless steel arch has an observation deck on the top which features a spectacular view.

Below: A winter scene on a farm in Porter County, Indiana, near Valparaiso.

The sunset casts its glow on the waters of the Ohio River near the town of Madison, Indiana.

Above: Benjamin Harrison's house in Indianapolis, Indiana, was built 15 years before he was elected President of the United States. Today it is a state memorial, containing 16 rooms with their original furniture.

Below: The 14-room cedar log house where Gene Stratton Porter lived for 20 years can be found in Limberlost State Memorial, near Geneva, Indiana. She was the author of the Hoosier classic *Girl of the Limberlost*.

Above: The James Whitcomb Riley house in Indianapolis at 528 Lockerbie Street. The Hoosier Poet lived here from 1892 until 1916, and the interior has been maintained in the same condition.

Below: The Culberson Mansion in New Albany, Indiana, is now a state memorial. Located at 914 East Main Street, it was built in 1869 for the then astronomical cost of $120,000.

Above: The Springs Valley Electric Railroad Trolley at French Lick, Indiana. It operates out of the old Monon Railroad station at the site of an old French trading post with its nearby salt lick.

Below: The Auburn-Cord-Duesenberg Museum in Auburn, Indiana, contains more than 130 of these and other classic cars, located in the original showroom of the Auburn Automobile Company.

Above: The *Belle of Louisville*, the old sternwheel riverboat, photographed on the Ohio River at Madison. In the middle of the nineteenth century, Madison was the largest city in Indiana — 5000 people.

Below: Old canal boats pulled by horses still travel along the Whitewater Canal at Metamora — but only for tourists. Canals were important in nineteenth century Indiana, for transporting goods and people.

Above: The Mississippi River with St Paul, Minnesota in the background. Barge traffic on the Mississippi is steady and voluminous with all types of raw materials being hauled by water.

Left: The Alexander Ramsey House on South Exchange Street in St Paul. This Victorian house was built in 1872 and was the home of Alexander Ramsey, governor, senator and secretary of war under President Rutherford B Hayes. It is open to the public and contains the original interior and the handsome furnishing.

Opposite: The Conservatory in Como Park, St Paul. The 443-acre park contains the Conservatory, a 70-acre lake and a zoo. The Conservatory contains permanent tropical and changing seasonal plant and flower exhibits, plus a 'gates ajar' floral display.

Overleaf: The Piper Tower in Minneapolis, Minnesota. This 44-story building with its glass facade rises to a height of 579 feet.

Left: A small herd of buffalo can be seen in Blue Mounds State Park near Luverne in Rock County, Minnesota. The 1380-acre park has as its main feature a three-mile long quartzite bluff called Blue Mound. According to the legend, Indians drove herds of buffalo off this mound to their deaths, then harvested their skins.

Opposite: The Courthouse in Jackson, Minnesota. Hostile Indians twice descended from the timber hills to this peaceful community on the banks of the Des Moines River. There is a monument to the slain settlers of the Sioux raiders in 1857 located in Ahsley Park. The courthouse contains a rock fossil and Indian Museum. South of Jackson is Fort Belmont, a replica of a civilian fort built for protection from these bands of renegade Indians. It features a sod house, which was the common first home for prairie settlers, a water-wheel-operated flour mill, a log chapel and other buildings and Indian artifacts.

Below: The sod house at Fort Belmont, southern Minnesota.

Overleaf: Fall foliage in Voyageurs National Park. About 80,000 acres of Minnesota's first national park are lakes and streams, ideal for canoeing and sailing.

FOURTH ST

SHERMAN ST

Previous spread: A houseboat plies the clear waters in Voyageurs National Park near International Falls. This park in the forested lake country of Minnesota features camping, boating, backpacking and fishing. About 219,000 of its acres are on the Canadian border.

Left: The North West Company Fur Post at Pine City in the Arrowhead region of Minnesota. This state historic site is a reconstructed fur trade outpost, based on archeological findings and old manuscripts. Here costumed guides explain the lifestyles and interactions of the traders, Voyageurs and Indians as there were in an early 1800s trading post.

Opposite top: The United States Hockey Hall of Fame (on Hat Trick Avenue) in Eveleth, Minnesota. It honors Americans who have contributed to the sport as players, coaches and administrators. The areas of the museum are devoted to high school, amateur, college, professional and international hockey, plus the two gold medal United States hockey teams.

Opposite bottom: The Smokey the Bear Statue in Municipal Park at the northwest edge of the International Falls business district. This is a giant symbol of the campaign against forest fires.

Below: The Arrowhead Region, as is all of Minnesota, is famous for its dairy products. Here is the aging room in one of the many cheese factories.

UNITED STATES HOCKEY HALL OF FAME

SMOKEY

SMOKEY

SMOKEY SAYS

Left: Mount Rushmore National Memorial. The faces of Washington, Jefferson, Theodore Roosevelt and Lincoln were carved in the granite mountain by Gutzon Borglum. Each head is 60 feet from chin to forehead.

Opposite top: The exotic rock formations in the Dells of the Wisconsin River.

Opposite bottom: The shores of Lake Superior in Minnesota. Superior, like all the Great Lakes, is a freshwater sea. But with its 31,700 square mile area, it is second in size only to the Caspian Sea.

Below: A view of the frozen Manitou River near Lake Superior in Minnesota.

Left: Wildflowers grow in the forest in Palisades-Kepler State Park, Iowa.

Above: A whitetail buck in Indiana's Brown County State Park.

Right: A rock formation in the Wisconsin Dells near Madison, Wisconsin.

Below: Fog forms when water from Greer Spring, Missouri, hits warm air.

Previous spread: A Wisconsin farm, nestled in the rolling hills of Sauk County in southern Wisconsin, is set aglow in the late afternoon sun.

Opposite: A man sells home grown flowers and plants at Madison's colorful farmer's market. Every Saturday during the summer months, farmers and artisans gather around the star-shaped Capitol building to sell their produce and crafts. Street performers stage all kinds of shows on the Capitol steps, entertaining passersby and contributing to the lively and sunny atmosphere of the market.

Left and below: Winter and summer form the backdrops for two idyllic farm settings in southern Wisconsin. Though the state is best known as 'America's Dairyland', northern Wisconsin is a wilderness which has remained untouched since the French explorers. In search of the fabled Northwest Passage, Frenchman Jean Nicolet landed at Green Bay on Wisconsin's Michigan shore in 1634. The native Winnebagoes who greeted him did not shower great riches on him as he expected, and it was not until 1856 that the French returned, this time to exploit the Wisconsin forests for furs. Logging later became the region's source of wealth and the Finnish settled there in great numbers, perhaps because the region was so similar to their homeland.

Top: Sunset over the North Dakota Badlands in the South Unit of Theodore Roosevelt National Park.

Above: The deep waters of Sylvan Lake in South Dakota's Black Hills National Park are fringed by thick forests of a variety of coniferous trees, whose extraordinary ebon hue gives the region its name. Extending over one and a quarter million acres, the park offers spectacular scenery and many recreational activities.

Left: Sunrise over Painted Canyon in the Badlands of the South Unit of Theodore Roosevelt National Park. Much of the area is composed of blue bentonite clay.

Opposite: The quiet beauty of a farmstead near Ellsworth, Wisconsin, as seen in the last days of fall.

Below: Millions of years of wind-and-water erosion and powerful earth convulsions have given the Pinnacles region in South Dakota's Badlands its phantasmagoric landscape. The land's wealth is in its many fossils, which are invaluable to the paleontological world.

Right: The Badlands' special beauty lies in the desolation and barrenness of the land, but the name accurately describes a few of the dangerous animals which inhabit the region, of which this rattlesnake, ready to defend itself, is a prime example.

Opposite top: The conical spire is a typical formation of the Badlands

as are deep ravines carved by rivers, sharp cones and ridges, and the many grotesque rock formations found in this jagged and desolate area. It is hard to believe that thousands of centuries ago the Badlands were a monotonous, flat grassland.

Opposite bottom: Once the mighty mammoth and the fierce saber-toothed tiger inhabited the Badlands. Nowadays only a few remaining bison roam the windswept land along with the odd coyote, prairie dog, rattlesnake, and rock wren or cliff swallow. Custer State Park, where the largest herds of bison can be seen, borders the state of Montana in South Dakota's northwestern corner.

Left: The ubiquitous prairie dog, here eating a twig, lives in large groups called towns. At a warning bark, all citizens dive underground.

Right: Central Kansas prairie. Native Tallgrass prairies, once a dominant feature of the Midwest, still grace many parts of Kansas.

Below: The mountain lion is still found in the Dakotas. Most spend the days in caves or hollow trees and hunt by night.

Far right: Granite spires in the Black Hills of South Dakota are known as 'The Needles.' Sacred to the Indians, the Black Hills contain gold fields and a variety of game.

Above: Wall Drug in Wall, South Dakota, is the hub of this small but progressive town. In the Hustead family since 1931, the drugstore's claim to fame came in 1936 when Dorothy Hustead advertised free ice water along the highway. Her innovative signs brought business back to the community which had severely felt the Depression. Now including a gift shop and cafe, Wall Drug can attract over 10,000 tourists in a single day during the summer.

Opposite: The Corn Palace in Mitchell, South Dakota. One hundred thousand ears of corn and over 2000 bushels of grain decorate the outer walls of the palace with elaborate renditions of farming life. Mitchell's first Corn Palace was erected in 1892 to display the community's wealth and attract settlers to the area. The present structure dates back to 1921 and occupies an entire city block. The decorations are changed annually after the harvest and it takes about two and a half months to complete them.

Left: The Tulip Festival Monument in Pella, southcentral Iowa, shelters the community's Christmas tree in winter but presides over the Tulip Festival each May. Founded in 1847, Pella became the home of eight hundred Hollanders who successfully settled the region. The Tulip Festival, replete with native garb and pageantry, traditional foods and entertainment, celebrates the community's Dutch heritage.

Opposite top: The town square in Pella, Iowa, is where the town's annual Tulip Festival is held each May. The picturesque and colorful buildings house traditional Dutch bakeries, delicatessens and shops.

Opposite bottom: The Herbert Hoover National Historic Site, west of Davenport, Iowa, features the two-room Hoover Birthplace Cottage. Restored in 1938, the cottage was originally built in 1871. A replica of the blacksmith shop run by the president's father sits behind the cottage.

Above: The Capitol building in Des Moines, Iowa, is an impressive Italian Renaissance structure which is the pride of the state. The 23-carat gold dome is the largest one in the country and stands 275 feet high overlooking the Des Moines River.

Left: Cattle wait to be sold in the mazelike stockyards of Omaha, Nebraska. Omaha's stockyards are one of the largest in the country, making Omaha the cattle market center for much of the west.

Above: The 800-foot high Scott's Bluff acted as a milestone for pioneers traveling west on the Oregon Trail along the North Platte River Valley. It was named in 1829 for the frontiersman Hiram Scott who suffered lethal injuries on a tracking expedition and died at the bluff.

Right: The Stuhr Museum of the Prairie Pioneer in Grand Island, Nebraska, showcases the original buildings of a nineteenth century prairie town. Settlements like this one sprang up along the Platte River Valley as pioneers headed west on the Oregon, Mormon or Lewis and Clark trails.

Far right: A young boy enjoys the freedom of summer playing in an old abandoned barn in Nebraska's lovely countryside.

The late afternoon sun accents this barn and silo in
Morton County, North Dakota.

Sunset near New River, Arizona. The giant
Saguaro cactus in the foreground produces a
bloom that is Arizona's state flower.

The Southwest and Southern California

One of the arches in Arches National Park near Moab, Utah. In the background are the snow-capped peaks of the La Sal Mountains.

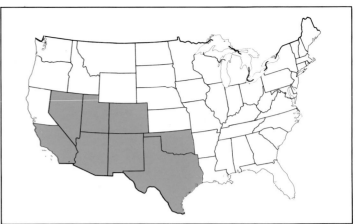

THE SOUTHWEST AND SOUTHERN CALIFORNIA

The Southwest contains seven states—Oklahoma, Texas, New Mexico, Arizona, Nevada, Utah and Colorado, plus Southern California. Most of the Southwest was once consigned to the Indians as worthless, but today it is a rich, varied and interesting region, growing more rapidly than that of any other part of the country.

This is not to say that the wide open spaces are disappearing. The magnificent vistas in which formations 50 miles away seem near at hand are still there. Bald, 12,000-foot-high mountains fringed with thick ponderosa pine and aspen forests rise within sight of the awe-inspiring, mile-deep Grand Canyon. Jagged, twisted lava beds spewed out by now-extinct volcanoes scar terrain that edges flowering meadows. Mesquite groves crowd spiny cacti while palm leaves fan back-yard patios. Earth-moving rivers like the Colorado and the Rio Grande—plus scores of sky-blue, man-made lakes and a few natural ones—water some of the most arid landscape in North America. Sand dunes, waterfalls, hot springs, geysers, salt flats, earthquake faults, glaciers and natural bridges are among the wonders of this region, whose lowest point is in Death Valley (282 feet below sea level) and whose highest point is more than 14,000 feet at Mount Whitney in California and Mount Elbert in Colorado.

Aside from an occasional fur trapper or explorer, the northern part of this region belonged to the Indians until well into the nineteenth century. Two major elements contributed to the wave of colonization near the middle of that century: the Mormon emigration and a succession of gold and silver strikes.

The southern part of this region was explored earlier. In 1540, a year after Friar Marcos de Niza had made a preliminary exploration into Arizona and New Mexico, Coronado led an expedition in search of the fabled Seven Cities of Cibola. Coronado did not find them, of course, but he laid the foundation for Spanish rule over the region for nearly three centuries.

Today, where Spanish conquistadores once vainly searched for gold and where French-Canadian trappers took pelts, fabulous bonanzas of oil and gas flow from the ground. Where hard-riding cowboys once herded cattle on the Long Drive, space scientists work on the frontier of technology.

Left: The Alamo is in downtown San Antonio. It was the site of the battle between Santa Anna and the Texans—1836.

Below left: The serpentine San Antonio River flows through the heart of the city. This is the River Walk.

This picture: The moon over downtown Dallas.

Left: The 118-foot Reunion Tower on its 10-acre landscaped site is the most striking recent arrival to Dallas' downtown skyline in Texas. At night the tower's dome, or 'moon,' beams computer-controlled patterns to delight the earthbound onlooker.

Above: Part of Dealy Plaza, the site of the assassination of President John F Kennedy, is now the Kennedy Memorial. Nearby, a 30-foot cenotaph surrounds an imposing block of black granite. Across from the former Texas School Book Depository building, the John F Kennedy Museum houses memorabilia of the tragedy.

Right: Thanksgiving Square, in downtown Dallas, typifies the modern look and feel of this well-planned metropolis. Dallas, unlike most Texas towns, has no history of battles, invasions, or shootouts. The city engaged a planning engineer early in the century to direct its growth.

Above: One of the many events of the annual Houston Festival in Texas, which takes place during the last two weeks of March. Centered at the Civic Center, events throughout the city celebrate city heritage.

Right: Houston's sprawling freeways, known affectionately as the 'Spaghetti Bowl,' lead to and from the futuristic buildings of the nation's third busiest port and fourth largest city.

Bottom left: The Houston Livestock Show and Rodeo takes place late February and early March at the Astrodome, and remains a major attraction in this modern city famous for cotton production, oil refining, and space exploration.

Top left: The Astros face the Braves at the Houston Astrodome. A marvel of modern technology, the unique all-weather structure can seat 45,000 to 66,000 spectators, depending on the event. An 18-story building would fit comfortably under the dome.

Right: The Houston Rockets take off. Reflecting the competitive spirit of a city fascinated by its own growth, professional, amateur, and collegiate sports thrive in Texas' major metropolis.

Above: Kemah Seabrook in Galveston County, between Houston and Galveston, is typical of a number of small towns and fishing communities clustered around and between refineries and shipping points in this part of coastal Texas. The beauty of the coastline and the rich fishing in the Gulf — shrimp, oysters, drum, sea trout and snapper — draw Texans and visitors from all over the Southwest.

Left: Yacht basin with Corpus Christi skyline in the background. Called a 'small village of smugglers and lawless men with but few women and no ladies' in 1846, Corpus Christi, on Texas' coast, soon prospered from ranching west of town, then gas and oil and now from modern space-age industries. Its bay is an excellent harbor with shipping channels to the Gulf.

Right: Sunset from Mustang Island. Mustang and Padre Islands are vast barriers of sand that separate the Gulf of Mexico from the Texas mainland. Padre Island, much of which is a National Seashore, was once the haunt of pirates, and is the graveyard of many shrimpers and larger vessels that have been swept ashore by treacherous Gulf winds and currents.

Opposite: Austin's state capitol building, made of pink granite from nearby Marble Falls. Austin, Texas, was also capital of the Republic.

Below: The 307-foot tower and fountain of the University of Texas, in downtown Austin.

Above: The tower of the Main Building at the University of Texas, rising 27 stories, is frequently lit in the university's orange and white. The orange top here indicates a winning game. In 1966 a demented student firing from the top of the tower shot and killed 14 persons and wounded 32.

Above: The guest house at the King Ranch, Kingsville, in the coastal plains region of Texas. The largest privately owned ranch in the world, it was established with a purchase of land by steamboat Captain Richard King in 1853. Today hundreds of cowboys tend Herefords, Shorthorns, Brahmans and the Kings' own breed, Santa Gertrudis, on the 823,400-acre spread.

Right: LBJ Ranch, Texas. The late President Lyndon B Johnson's Hereford ranch, still a working property near Johnson City, is now a National Historical Park. During Johnson's administration the ranch became known as the Texas White House. Nearby, on the Pedernales River, the LBJ State Historical Park features a living museum of buffalo and Texas longhorn cattle.

Left: Central Park, Laredo, Texas. A city on the Rio Grande where date palms, oleanders, bougainvillaea and palmettos line the residential streets, Laredo is the most important US rail depot to Mexico and is also on the Pan American Highway. The border town has lived under seven flags, including its own Republic of the Rio Grande.

Left: Plants adapted to storing water are representative of lowlands growth in the Big Bend area of Texas. These cacti, with nearby wildflowers and scrub, grow in a region of Big Bend called the Basin, a huge bowl at the foot of Casa Grande Mountain which is also the principal tourist center for the huge national park.

Right: Evening Star, Big Bend. The scenery and wildlife of this vast park are more typical of Mexico than of the American southwest. Camels were tried here by the US Cavalry in 1859-60 with excellent results, but experiments were interrupted by the Civil War, after which camels were soon rendered obsolete by railroads.

Below: Aptly named Cold and Barren, this area is typical of the rugged beauty of Big Bend. High in its mountain canyons are forests of Ponderosa pine, Douglas fir, and Arizona cypress. The misty Chisos Mountains take their name from the Apache word for ghostly or the Comanche word for echo.

Downtown El Paso, with Ciudad Juarez, Mexico, in the background. The border between the two towns is at midstream of the Rio Grande.

Top: Despite the ascendancy of the internal combustion engine, nothing can replace the cowboy and his skillful mount for many Texan ranching duties.

Above: The Western Diamondback rattlesnake is as beautiful as it is deadly. Its ominous warning sound is feared by men and animals alike.

Right: These longhorns near Nacogdoches, Texas, are kept as pets. Animal husbandry has developed superior strains for beef.

Far right: The caprock canyons of Texas' Briscoe County are a living text for geologists.

Above: Tulsa, the largest city in eastern Oklahoma, is one of the oil capitals of the world and has enjoyed much prosperity as a result. But, true to the pioneer spirit that shaped this state, Tulsa is looking ahead at new and innovative techniques to produce energy.

Right: A typical rural scene unfolds near Verden, Oklahoma. The brick-red earth was prized by the Choctaw Indians who inhabited the area and called the land 'home of the red man.' A unique feature of Oklahoma — sadly the result of massive forced relocations from 1835 to the late 1880s — is the high numbers of Indians living in this state.

Above: Moonrise over Santa Fe, New Mexico. Founded by Spaniards about 1610 on an old Indian pueblo, Santa Fe, the capital of New Mexico, is said to be the oldest seat of government in America. It is situated on a high rolling tableland dotted with piñon pines and backed by the lofty Sangre de Cristo Mountains.

Left: The Rio Chama flows through a mountain valley in northern New Mexico to join the Rio Grande.

Below: Adobe buildings at Taos Pueblo, New Mexico. These multi-storied communal dwellings are located on a high plateau flanked by the Sangre de Cristo Mountains which rise to 13,161 feet at nearby Wheeler Peak, the highest elevation in the State of New Mexico. Also nearby are the ruins of the Mission of San Geronimo de Taos, founded in 1610.

Part of the 226-square-mile sea of gypsum sand dunes at White Sands National Monument southwest of Alamagordo, New Mexico.

Top: Buckwheat grows on a ledge on Cape Royal on the Grand Canyon's North Rim at the bottom of the Walhala Plateau.

Above: A twilight view of some more ledges at Bright Angel Point on the North Rim near the Grand Canyon Lodge.

Left: A panoramic view of the stately Grand Canyon, Arizona.

Top and above: Petrified logs in Jasper Forest National Park, near Holbrook, Arizona. Some of the petrified logs with root systems still attached indicate that they grew nearby.

Right: Blue Mesa, Arizona, in the morning. This area's delicately colored and banded buttes, mesas and cones clearly reveal the ancient layers of the floodplain it once was. The tree trunks were petrified as a result of the silica-bearing ground waters that seeped through the wood tissues replacing them with silica deposits, which then hardened, petrifying the wood.

Above: A Navajo woman and child dressed in the traditional velvet clothes and turquoise jewelry, ride through scenic Monument Valley which borders the Navajo-Hopi Indian reservation in Arizona. Navajo and Hopi Indians have shared this land for hundreds of years and are both considered the most traditional Indian tribes left in the United States, living as their ancestors did.

Left: A view of the Old Town in Albuquerque, New Mexico. In the background is the famous Church of San Felipe that possesses an unusual spiral staircase built around an ancient and sacred spruce tree. Mass has been said in the Church of San Felipe every day since its doors first opened in 1706.

Opposite: Known as the 'White Dove of the Desert,' Mission San Xavier del Bac near Tucson, Arizona, was founded around 1700 and is a gem of Spanish colonial architecture.

Left: The dramatic Canyon de Chelly in Arizona is now a national monument. This impressive preserve, where sheer, red sandstone walls rise as high as a thousand feet above the canyon floor and gigantic formations stand taller than an 80-story building, shows Indian civilization from the early Anasazi Period, about 350 AD, through thirteenth-century cliff dwellings. When William of Normandy defeated the English at the Battle of Hastings in 1066, Pueblo Indians had already built dwellings in these walls.

Opposite: Monument Valley covers several thousand square miles on both sides of the Utah-Arizona state line. It has become famous for its giant red sandstone monoliths and spires rising several thousand feet above the surrounding plains of the Navajo Reservation. This colorful valley with the sandstone pillars and spires that resemble huge temple ruins has often been the site of moving picture location camps. Director John Ford used it many times for the background for his western films, often starring John Wayne.

Below: Red Rock Crossing near Sedona, Arizona. Located in Oak Creek Canyon, which begins south of Flagstaff and continues for a dozen miles to Sedona, the canyon opens up into a gorgeous, rock-rimmed amphitheater that has also been used as a background for many Western movies. The stream is spectacular, especially for fishermen.

Above: The Cliff Palace was the first major Anasazi dwelling to be discovered, in Mesa Verde National Park, Colorado. It was found by local cowboys about a century ago, and contains more than 200 living rooms, 23 kivas (kiva is a Hopi word for 'ceremonial room'), and numerous storage rooms.

Right: A panoramic view of the Cliff Palace, which is estimated to have been built in the mid 1200s.

Below: These evocative painted designs are found throughout the southwest and reveal the existence of an ancient Indian civilization in the region.

Previous spread: Rocky Mountain National Park, near Estes, Colorado, sits astride the Continental Divide. It is a land of snow-capped mountain ranges, sparkling lakes, pine and fir and quaking aspen, elk, deer and bighorn sheep. Trail Ridge Road, a wide and beautiful highway, crosses the park and drops down the west side of the Divide to Grand Lake. Among many other sights, the Mummy Range, the Never Summer Range, Iceberg Lake and Specimen Mountain are seen from the Trail Ridge Road.

Above: The towering 12,000-foot-high San Francisco Peaks can be seen from Coconino National Forest near Flagstaff, Arizona. The forest surrounds the city of Flagstaff, and Arizona's highest point, Humphreys Peak, is here, as is Lake of Cinders, a 640,000 square-foot moonscape that was created by the United States Geological Survey. Other outstanding scenic areas include parts of the Mogollon Rim and the Verde River Valley, part of the Sycamore Canyon Wilderness area, extinct volcanoes and lava beds. This is where Zane Grey wrote his novel, *Call of the Canyon.*

Opposite: In this tight, peak-rimmed valley near Silverton, Colorado, one can see the Needle Mountains in the Rocky Mountain chain.

Right: The Twin Falls in the Yankee Boy Basin in the Colorado Rockies near Ouray lie in a natural basin surrounded by the 12,000 to 13,000-foot peaks of the San Juan Mountains of the Rocky Mountain chain.

276

Left: A farm in Gunnison County, Colorado sits at the foot of the snowcapped and spectacular Rocky Mountains.

Above: The Brown Palace Hotel on the corner of Tremont and 17th Streets in Denver, Colorado, is the West's most renowned hotel.

Overleaf: The glorious yellow of aspens in autumn is reflected in the dark waters of Maroon Lake, near Aspen, Colorado.

279

'Landscape Arch' at sunrise, in the Devil's Garden area of Arches National Park, Utah, is an awesome sight.

Opposite: The Navajo Loop Trail, one and a half miles long, after a January snowstorm, Bryce Canyon National Park, Utah.

Above: A view of Silent City from Inspiration Point in Bryce Canyon. Boat Mesa is in the background, reflecting the morning sun.

Left: A spectacular waterfall in Zion National Park, Utah. The trees in the foreground are cottonwoods and are located in The Temple of Sinawava, a natural amphitheater.

Opposite top right: The Virgin River in Zion Canyon. This placid stream may become a raging torrent during spring runoffs and after a sudden summer storm, depositing debris at every turn — logs, rocks and other materials from many miles distant. Thus it is an important erosion force.

Opposite top left: The lush valley of the Fremont River in Capitol Reef National Park, Utah. This is the area where Indians, native to the region, once grew their crops.

Opposite bottom: The Three Patriarchs in Zion Canyon.

Below: The West Temple, Towers of the Virgin.

Top: About 40,000 tons of salt are harvested annually from 1,500-square-mile Great Salt Lake, Utah. One of the natural wonders of the world, the lake is about six times as salty as the ocean.

Above: The red sandstone cliffs, crisp blue skies and deep blue waters of the 150,000 acre Lake Powell form the spectacular scenery of the Lake Powell region in southeastern Utah.

Opposite: Salt Lake City's Main Street features the single most important shrine of Mormonism, the Mormon Temple, whose 200-foot spires are aglow in the night.

Left: The world-famous Lake Tahoe in Nevada, second in altitude and size only to Lake Titicaca in South America, has been praised for its startling blue and clear waters and is thought by many to be the world's most spectacular freshwater lake.

Above: The moon rises over nature's magnificent red and yellow sandstone sculptures in Valley of Fire State Park, Nevada. Indians inhabited this region around 1500 BC and left stunning petroglyphs carved on these rocks.

Top: Reno, 'The Biggest Little City in the World,' north of Lake Tahoe in Nevada, is a little 'Las Vegas' with fine restaurants, many casino-hotels and excellent live entertainment.

Above: Downtown Las Vegas, Nevada, in the early morning. The largest city in the state, it spreads over a desert plain east of the Charleston Range. Big, brassy, and aglow with neon lighting, Las Vegas is a round-the-clock, year-round resort. Its bars and casinos—with roulette wheels, slot machines, crap and poker games, faro, chuckaluck and other games of chance—operate 24 hours a day. Luxurious hotels on the 'Strip' stage elaborate shows for their customers.

Left: The living is easy—and expensive—in Palm Springs, California.

Below: The highest dam in the world—Hoover Dam, near Las Vegas.

Above: Looking upwards at giant sequoias in the morning fog — Giant Forest of Sequoia National Park, California.

Right: 'The Senate,' a group of sequoia trees in Congress Grove, Sequoia National Park. Few records show mature sequoias ever having died of disease or insect attack. They usually die by being toppled by the wind or a bolt of lightning.

Opposite: Rare but heavy rainstorms in the desert cause flash floods, which in turn erode the dry washes such as this one, seen running through the mudstone hills below Zabriskie Point in Death Valley, California.

This spread: The sights of San Diego include beaches such as the one at La Jolla, above, the mission San Diego de Alcala, right, and California Tower in Balboa Park, opposite. Below, the city's modern skyline forms a backdrop for the boats riding at anchor in the harbor.

Above and below: Marineland of the Pacific in Palos Verdes treats visitors to live shows featuring killer whales, dolphins, and porpoises.

Opposite top and bottom: Cinderella's castle and the nightly fireworks show are the highlight of a trip to Disneyland, which is connected to the Disneyland Hotel by the monorail, in Anaheim, California.

Left: Two young visitors are greeted by a favorite Disney character on Disneyland's Main Street USA.

Above: The buildings of downtown Los Angeles as viewed from the Harbor Freeway. Directions and locations in Los Angeles are reckoned in terms of the freeways, whose names include the Golden State, the Santa Monica, the Hollywood, the Ventura, the Santa Ana and the San Diego. **Opposite:** The famous Hollywood sign towers over villas and mansions in Hollywood Hills, Los Angeles.

Left: The coastline at Los Angeles. Land is so expensive here that individual house lots are quite small, and waterfront property is at a premium.

Opposite: A scenic view of suburban homes at Hollywood Reservoir in Los Angeles. The city began as a sleepy Spanish village. On 4 September 1781 Don Felipe de Neve, Governor of California, marched to the site of the present city and with solemn ceremonies founded 'The Town of Our Lady the Queen of the Angels of Porciuncula' — now shortened to 'Los Angeles.' The city grew to its present enormous size in relatively recent years, partly by absorbing neighboring communities. One of these was Hollywood, legendary center of the film industry and modern television production. In the half-century between 1890 and 1940, the city grew from 50,395 to 1,504,277 — a gain of 2,645.7 percent. It now has almost three million residents.

Below: Los Angeles at night. Los Angeles is the largest city in the United States in area and second largest in population in its metropolitan area. Spreading for miles inland and along the ocean, this great city is the center of far-flung orange groves and of an important oil-producing area. It is rich in manufactures, with a fine harbor, and its superb beaches are an unexcelled resort attraction.

Overleaf: A view of Marina Del Rey in the heart of the Los Angeles County coastline. The three counties of Southern California have more boat berths than any other county and among them have nearly half of the state's total.

Top: Southern California gave a rousing welcome to the USA teams as they entered the LA Memorial Coliseum for the 1984 Summer Olympics.

Above: Set amidst the beautiful Hollywood Hills, the Hollywood Bowl is used for both classical and pop concerts.

Opposite: Rolls-Royces and Mercedes Benzes line up in front of the exclusive Beverly Hills hotel in Los Angeles.

Above: Mission Santa Barbara was founded by the early Spanish colonists as part of a whole archipelago of outposts along the California southern coast, and gave its name to the present-day city.

Top: William Randolph Hearst's enormous castle at San Simeon.

Left: Youngsters investigate the wonders of teeming coastal tide pools on Santa Barbara's coast.

Opposite: The Seventeen-Mile Drive between Carmel and Monterey via Pebble Beach is the Golden State's only toll road. The toll is moderate but the views are priceless.

A breathtaking vista from the cliffs of Big Sur.

White sandy beaches and gnarled cypress help make Carmel one of the most photographed scenes on California's coastline.

The Northwest and Northern California

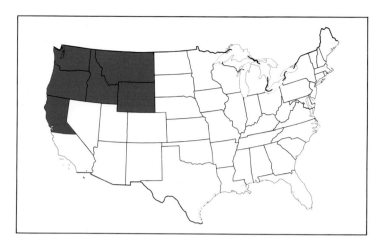

THE NORTHWEST AND NORTHERN CALIFORNIA

There are five states — Oregon, Washington, Idaho, Montana and Wyoming — in the Northwest, plus Northern California. Few regions in the world can match this area for variety and number of natural wonders — a rain forest wilderness, groves of giant trees, glaciers, raging rivers flowing through deep gorges, great craggy mountain peaks, active volcanoes, scorching deserts.

It is one of the most productive regions of the world. In Northern California, Washington and Oregon are orchards, cattle ranges, limitless wheat fields. In Idaho, Montana and Wyoming are vast ranches and underground riches.

Exotic place names give clues to the region's historical background. In Northern California most of the major cities have Spanish names — San Francisco, Sacramento, San José. In other states there are reminders of the French fur trappers — Grand Coulee, Coeur d'Alene.

Dwellings and other structures tell the story of the land's settlement. The Spanish contributed the thick-walled, comfortable adobe houses. A New Englander in Monterey added galleries to a typical Yankee home and created the Monterey style. Russians descending the coast from Alaska built forts and churches. Chinese mine workers built joss houses and temples, French and Italian wine makers added stone wineries. Lumber barons and rich ranchers dotted the landscape with great Victorian mansions, while lumberjacks hewed out log cabins.

Previous spread: Horses graze in Grand Teton National Park, Wyoming. Its 485 square-miles include some of the most breathtaking landscape in North America. Within the park are the alpine-like, glacier-carved Grand Teton Mountains, with their jagged peaks and intervening canyons; a dozen glaciers; eight large lakes; extensive fir, spruce and pine forests and summits ranging from 11,000 to nearly 14,000 feet above sea level.

Right: Yellowstone Falls in Yellowstone National Park, Wyoming — the oldest and most noted of the federal preserves.

Below: The Riverside Geyser erupts — Upper Geyser Basin, Yellowstone National Park, Wyoming. Riverside shares the Upper Geyser Basin with Old Faithful, and the Grand, Castle and Beehive Geysers, among others. One of the most predictable in the park, Riverside erupts every five and three quarter hours.

Bottom: Firehole Falls in the morning. The Firehole River, on which the falls are located, passes through the Upper Geyser Basin quite near the geysers located there.

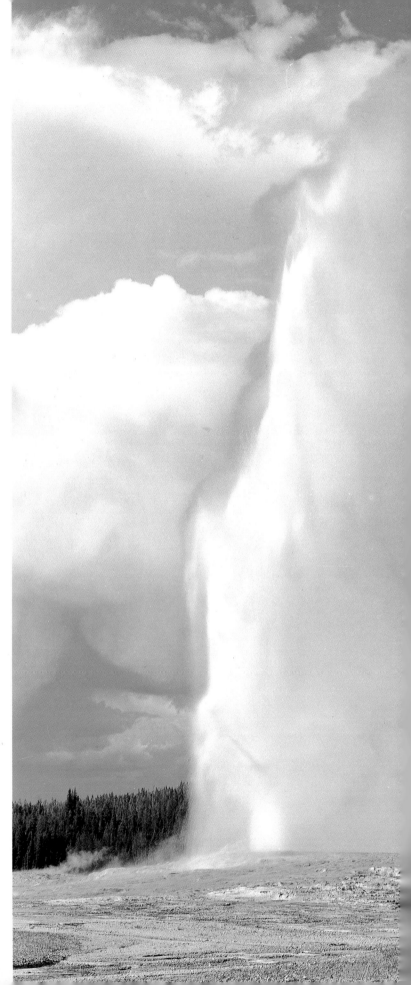

Left: An eruption of Old Faithful Geyser. Old Faithful erupts on an average of every 71 minutes, although this can vary from 33 to 148 minutes. Still, it is the star of Yellowstone National Park, Wyoming, since it hasn't missed a performance in the more than 100 years since its discovery.

Above: An eruption of the Great Fountain Geyser in Yellowstone National Park.

Above: Mount St John in the Teton Range in Grand Teton National Park, Wyoming. A morning view looking across Jackson Lake.

Right: A morning shot of String Lake with the mountains in the background. String Lake is actually not a lake at all; it is more like a natural passageway between Leigh Lake and Jenny Lake in Grand Teton National Park.

Far right: Snake River, which flows from the north to Jackson Lake and then exits the lake near its southern end, bisects the Grand Teton National Park. Here it is seen on a September morning.

Right: An adult bald eagle stands watch at the nest, set high in a treetop, in June in Grand Teton National Park, Wyoming. The bald eagle is the United States' national bird and is protected by a special act of Congress. Though only 30 to 43 inches long, the largest eagles spread their wings up to eight feet wide. Their diet consists primarily of fish, which is abundant in the many lakes and streams in the park.

Below: Sunrise over the Tetons in Grand Teton National Park, with a view from Schwabacher Landing on the Snake River in the foreground. Grand Teton National Park is filled with beautiful trees, the grandeur of the mountains, which range from 11,000 to nearly 14,000 feet above sea level, and spectacular wildlife. The Park is also the winter feeding ground for the largest American elk herd.

Above: Elk antlers crown the entrance to this saloon in Cody, Wyoming. This Old Trail town, named after the famous scout 'Buffalo Bill' Cody, is at an altitude of 5002 feet and stands much as it did when it was a roaring Western town. In July, visitors flock to the area for the famous Cody Stampede, the town's annual rodeo.

Opposite: A log cabin in the early morning sun, alone in the pristine snowy landscape of Montana's magnificent Rocky Mountains.

Left: Most of Montana was once Blackfoot Indian country. They fiercely defended their lands and the sacred bison from the onslaught of white men in search of fortunes until 1877, when they finally bowed to the inevitable. Today, in Browning, Montana, headquarters of the 2400-acre Blackfoot Indian Reservation, colorful pow-wows, replete with traditional dances and ceremonies, celebrate the region's Indian heritage on North American Indian Days.

Overleaf: A favorite destination in Glacier National Park, Montana, is the Hanging Gardens near Logan Pass, known for its brilliant display of wildflowers.

Right: A view in Glacier National Park, Montana, which has gorgeous scenery, clear mountain lakes, and active glaciers. Located on Montana's Canadian border, this 1600 square-mile park is a glacier-carved Rocky Mountain wonderland. The park has 60 small glaciers in the process of disappearing, and nearly 200 glacier-formed lakes. Alpine flowers can be found there, as well as white mountain goat, elk, moose, bighorn sheep, deer and bear.

Opposite: Rising Sun Mountain in Glacier National Park.

Below: The Many Glacier Hotel at Grinnell Point in Glacier National Park, overlooking Swiftcurrent Lake. Big, rugged and primitive, Glacier National Park is nature's unspoiled domain. Man and his civilization are reduced to insignificance by the wild grandeur of these million acres. Declared a national park on 11 May 1910, the park, with its spectacular scenery, is preserved year after year much as it was when Meriwether Lewis saw it in the distance in 1806. Therefore, it is easy to get lost, once off the trail, and some of the wild animals can be dangerous. This is a land where winter does not beat a full retreat until mid-June, and sometimes returns in mid-September. Snowbanks line the road in July.

Overleaf: A cluster of alpine-like houses crowd at the edge of a forest with the mighty Tetons for a backdrop, near Last Chance, Idaho, just across the Wyoming border. The Basque settled here in great numbers and the landscape is reminiscent of their homelands in the Pyrenees.

Below: Seaweed grows on the shore of Hood Canal west of Seattle, Washington.

Right: A windy day on St Mary Lake, Glacier National Park, Montana.

Bottom: Woodland caribou often range down from Canada into northern Idaho — as here — and Washington.

Opposite top: The jagged peaks of the Sawtooth Mountains in Idaho.

Opposite bottom: Alders flourish in the Mossy Fern Canyon of Redwood National Park, California.

Right: Mount Ranier, south of Seattle, Washington, rises from near sea level to 14,410 feet. It is a dormant volcano, and is the dominant natural feature of the State of Washington. It is located in Mount Rainier National Park, which also has permanent snow fields, high meadows, crystal clear lakes and a great variety of trees and flowers. The park is located in the Cascade Range of mountains.

Opposite: A scenic view in Olympic National Park, Washington. This occupies the heart of the Olympic Peninsula on the northwest coast of the state between the Pacific Ocean and Puget Sound. It is a vast area, having zones ranging from temperate rain forests to mountain glaciers, and it preserves native plant and animal life.

Below: Downtown Seattle, Washington, is dominated by the Space Needle (right). The needle, with its high observation deck, is located in Seattle Center, which was built for the 1962 Seattle World's Fair. Seattle is the metropolis of Washington and the Pacific Northwest. Its salt-water harbor of Elliott Bay is rimmed by port facilities for the largest ocean-going vessels. It has a fresh-water harbor for fishing and pleasure boats. Scenic boulevards link waterfronts with hilltops and provide views of distant mountains. Its industries are varied — lumbering, airplane manufacturing, aluminum fabrication, shipbuilding and others.

Fishing boats line the piers at Fisherman's Terminal in Seattle's harbor. The Puget Sound waters and the Pacific Ocean beyond provide abundant catches for this important local industry.

Previous spread: Aspen trees flourish throughout the northwestern Rockies and provide food for moose and beavers, two of the many animals that make this region their home.

Right: Sawtooth Ridge and Fisher Creek in North Cascades National Park, Washington.

Below: Giant fern shoots in North Cascades National Park with the mountains in the background. In this area can sometimes be seen mountain goats, deer, black bear, wolverines, martens, fishers, grizzly bear, cougar and moose. White-tailed ptarmigans and bald eagles as well as many other smaller birds can be occasionally spotted.

Right: The bighorn sheep with its characteristic thick spiralled horns makes its home in the high country of Glacier National Park, Montana, and elsewhere in the Rocky Mountains.

Below: Mountains of the North Cascades National Park, Washington. Exploration of the region began in 1814 when Alexander Ross crossed the present national park's southern border. A handful of explorers followed him over the years. They commented on the region's rugged, isolated nature. Miners prospected for gold, lead, zinc and platinum from 1880 to 1910. Some logging and homesteading occurred around 1900. Today the Skagit River, the area's main artery, is used to generate electricity.

Above: A view of Eagle Crags and the Phantom Ship formation on the southeast edge of Crater Lake, Oregon. The reason that the water is so blue is that light is absorbed color by color as it passes through clear water. First the red goes, then orange, yellow and green. The last to be absorbed is the blue. Only the deepest blue gets reflected back to the surface from 300 feet, the natural limit of penetration. Then it is seen as the color of the water. Actually the water is no more blue than the sky is blue.

Left: Another view of the Phantom Ship formation in Crater Lake — this time from the Sun Notch on Mount Thielsen at sunset.

Opposite far top: The barren and desolate 'banks' of Crater Lake are pure lava walls which rise 500 to 2000 feet high above the lake.

Opposite far bottom: A winter view of Wizard Island in Crater Lake. Wizard Island is actually a small extinct volcanic cone that built up after Mount Mazama collapsed to form the caldera in which Crater Lake and the island are located.

Left: Scotch broom, originally a native of Western Europe, grows here in southern Oregon's Bandon State Park along the Pacific Ocean.

Above: The green forest floor of the Salmon River Trail, one of the many trails that wind through Mount Hood National Forest in northern Oregon. This vast (1,115,327 acres) forest has numerous scenic attractions including hot springs, waterfalls, alpine meadows and lakes. Many of the trails are closed to vehicular traffic so that visitors can enjoy a true wilderness environment.

Right: At 11,245 feet Mount Hood is the highest peak in Oregon and is covered with snow throughout the entire year. It is in fact an old volcano that is not absolutely extinct — like Mount St Helens, only 60 miles to the north, in Washington. Mount Hood rises from the center of the National Forest named after it, with the attractions and activities revolving around its slopes.

Top: The Willamette River winds through Portland, Oregon, dividing the city's gracious residential area from the highrise buildings of downtown's commercial center. Mount Hood, with its summit lost in clouds, forms an imposing backdrop to this charming city.

Above: Haystack Rock at Cannon Beach is one of the Oregon shoreline's most spectacular sights, seen here breaking through the early morning mists. Cannon Beach was only a decade ago a sleepy coastal village and is now an arts colony bursting with activity.

Right: Many lighthouses dot Oregon's breathtaking coastline. This lighthouse, built in 1894, sits on the jutting Heceta Head, named for the early Spanish explorer Captain Bruno Heceta. Nearby are the Sea Lion Caves, in which lives a large herd of Stellar sea lions.

Top: The peak of the Transamerica pyramid is the crown jewel in San Francisco's nighttime skyline.

Above: The famous San Francisco fog creeps catlike over Twin Peaks and Mount Sutro.

Right: The Bay Bridge crosses Yerba Buena Island to connect Oakland with San Francisco, California.

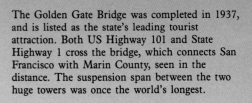

The Golden Gate Bridge was completed in 1937, and is listed as the state's leading tourist attraction. Both US Highway 101 and State Highway 1 cross the bridge, which connects San Francisco with Marin County, seen in the distance. The suspension span between the two huge towers was once the world's longest.

Above: Victorian houses are found in the older towns and cities around the San Francisco Bay. Built in the late nineteenth century, they survived the notorious 1906 earthquake and today are prized by homebuyers.

Below: The town of Sausalito, in Marin County, offers spectacular views of the Bay.

Below: Noe Valley, in the heart of San Francisco, takes on the look of a European village under the mantle of the rare snowfall that the city received in February 1976.

Opposite: Telegraph Hill, capped by the famous Coit Tower, is one of San Francisco's oldest and most prized residential areas.

Opposite: A California winery in the Napa Valley.

Above: A two-lane blacktop winds through Redwood National Park.
Below: Colorful flowers add a soft touch to a weathered home in Mendocino, California.

Right: A neoclassic statuary caps the century old Mendocino F&AM Lodge, California.

Above: Mount Shasta, the highest mountain in northern California, is a popular skiing area.

Top and right: Mount Lassen, seen here from the air in late winter and in midsummer reflected in Manzanita Lake, is the centerpiece of Lassen Volcanic National Park, California.

Overleaf: The redwood forests along California's northern coast have awed many a visitor.

Top: Boats huddle at the northern shore of Lake Tahoe, as snow dusts the peaks around the lake.

Left and above: Every winter many visitors from California's coastal cities drive to the High Sierra to ski and stay in places like Alpine Village, at left.

Opposite: An early morning frost turns an ordinary thistle into a beautiful and delicate crystal.

Above: The Ahwahnee, Yosemite Valley's grand hotel, offers comfortable rooms with spectacular views.

Top and right: The granite face of Half Dome Mountain is the dominant landmark in Yosemite Valley, California, and a veritable magnet as well for mountain climbers from all over the world.

Above: As sunshine washes into the stillness of Yosemite Valley, a light breath of mist rises off the icy Merced River.

Opposite: Yosemite Falls, the nation's tallest waterfall, grows into an immense, roaring vertical river as it is fed by melting snow higher in the mountains.

Mt McKinley, the highest mountain in North
America at 20,320 feet, and Mt Hunter, at 14,573
feet, tower over the Kahiltna Glacier in Alaska.

Alaska and Hawaii

ALASKA AND HAWAII

America's two newest states, Alaska (admitted in January 1959) and Hawaii (admitted in August 1959), are the only states that are not contiguous with the other 48.

Alaska is huge, its 585,412 square-miles being more than twice the size of the next largest state, Texas. But it ranks fiftieth in residents, with only a little more than 400,000 people.

Alaska's position on the globe is the most northern and western portion of the North American continent. Nome, Alaska, is farther west than Honolulu, Hawaii; Attu Island, the most western of the Alaskan Aleutian Island Chain, is as far west as New Zealand. In latitude, Juneau, Alaska is about the same distance north as Stockholm, Sweden; and Point Barrow, the northernmost point of the state, is about as far north as the North Cape in Norway.

Alaska was discovered in 1741 by Vitus Bering, a Danish navigator under contract to Tsar Peter the Great of Russia. In 1867, the United States Secretary of State William Seward offered Russia $7.2 million dollars for the vast wilderness, and the American flag was raised in Sitka on 18 October 1867.

Hawaii is the only state which is a group of islands. With the exception of South Florida, it is the only state with a subtropical climate. Discovered by Captain James Cook in 1778, they were originally called the Sandwich Islands. The US annexed Hawaii in 1898 and made it a territory in 1900.

Below left: Winstanley Creek in Misty Fjords National Monument near Ketchikan, Alaska.

This picture: Mount McLaughlin on the Kenai Peninsula, Alaska.

Right: A contestant tests his skill in the calf-roping competition during the rodeo in Soldotna. Located on the western coast of the Kenai Peninsula, Soldotna sponsors an annual Progress Days celebration in July, which includes the rodeo and a parade.

Below: Sea lions bask on the rocks in Kenai Fjords National Park. Established in 1980 and containing 587,000 acres of glaciers, mountains and steep fjords, the park is a breeding ground for the animals.

Opposite top: Two large male Alaskan brown bears fight over a strategic fishing spot in the McNeil River. The McNeil River State Game Sanctuary is located in the northern region of the Alaska Peninsula.

Opposite middle left: A brown bear and her cub wander through a valley field. Bears range widely in search of food.

Opposite bottom left: A coastal fox curled into napping position rests on a bed of moss near Katmai.

Opposite right: A colorful puffin in the Pribilofs north of the Aleutian chain.

The port city of Haines nestles on a wooded peninsula at the northern end of the Lynn Canal.

Previous spread: Anchorage, the hub of Alaska, is surrounded by mountains and situated on Cook Inlet on Alaska's Gulf Coast. Northeast of the city is the fertile Matanuska Valley, which now produces half of Alaska's crops.

Opposite top: Since Barrow's population is mainly Eskimo, it is considered the largest Eskimo village in Alaska, with a population of 2800. Although much of the town appears less than charming, with dirt streets and prefabricated houses, Barrow has been recently upgrading itself and has complex research facilities devoted to the study of Arctic ecology. The government's Distant Early Warning System started here.

Opposite below: A 1:30 am sunrise on pack ice in the Arctic Ocean near Barrow. While the shores at this northern latitude remain frozen in swells and ridges for seven to eight months of the year, break-up signals the start of the whale-hunting season.

Right: The crackling cold can practically be seen in this picture of Barrow at -45 degrees. Although winter temperatures average between this and 15 degrees above zero, summer temperatures range in the 40s and the summer sun does not set for 82 days.

Below: A nameless glacier winds its way through the jagged, treeless peaks of the Brooks Range. Extending from the coast to the Canadian border, the mountain range is from 50 to 100 miles wide.

A glacier calves icebergs into chilly waters.
Alaska's many glaciers were explored and
studied by the great naturalist John Muir.

Left: The blanket toss was originally perhaps a means for Eskimo hunters to spot game or to celebrate a successful whale hunt. Here it enlivens festivities at the annual Anchorage Fur Rendezvous in February. Other events include sportscar races on ice, dog sled races, Indian dances and a bear-judging contest.

Above: The World Championship Dog Sled Races during the Anchorage Fur Rendezvous begin and end in the city itself, and run through 25 grueling miles of back country. Many mushers represent communities or villages that have pooled their best dogs and funds to send a competitor to these races.

Right: Farewells are said at the dock where a float plane readies for take-off from the Kenai Peninsula. Bush planes are a practical and common way to travel in Alaska, and provide some of the best sightseeing in remote areas. With most of the state not accessible by road, a large number of Alaskans fly their own planes.

Left: The stately Governor's Mansion in Juneau was built in 1912. This white-pillared colonial is located near other State buildings.

Top left: The Fourth of July celebration in Juneau, complete with parade and carnival, displays Alaska's pride in being the 49th state.

Top right: The colorful lights of Juneau at night reflect in the Gastineau Channel. This bustling city is especially lively during the winter legislative session.

Above: A dramatic view through an ice cave in the Mendenhall Glacier. Located 13 miles north of Juneau, the glacier is a mile and a half wide.

Right: A dusting of snow creates a picturesque scene in downtown Juneau.

Coconut trees fringe the black sand beach of Kaimu on Hawaii's eastern shore, formed as molten lava met the ocean and exploded into pieces.

Below: Clouds drift lazily over the crater of Diamond Head and Waikiki, as a boat heads back to harbor after a morning cruise.

Bottom: Built in 1927, the Sheraton Royal Hawaiian Hotel quickly became one of the most popular resorts in the islands. The Pink Palace, with its exquisite setting and period decor, still woos many an island guest.

Right: Both the Waikiki and Hawaii yacht clubs are located in the picturesque Ala Wai Yacht Basin.

Top: Makapuu Beach at Honolulu's eastern end is a favorite spot for body-surfing and escaping from the crowds at Waikiki. The flat island offshore is called Kaohikaipu Island; the larger one is Manana, also known as Rabbit Island.

Above: The traditional *luau* is an integral part of Hawaiian social life. The pig, filled with heated rocks and wrapped in leaves, is buried with fish and yams in a hole lined with wood and steaming lava rock. Hours later the food, distinctly flavored, is unearthed and served.

Left: Surfing is one of Hawaii's most popular sports today, as it was among the ancient Hawaiians, who loved to race and place bets on surfers. In the summer, surfing is best on Hawaii's south shores. The excitement and challenge of this incomparable sport is obviously addictive.

Above: Sailing is one of the best and most relaxing ways to appreciate Hawaii's beauty — tacking in an ocean breeze, skimming over sapphire-blue water, feeling the salty spray.

Below: Water skiing isn't the only type of skiing on Hawaii, as snow skiing reaches a new height on Mauna Kea's whitecapped peak.

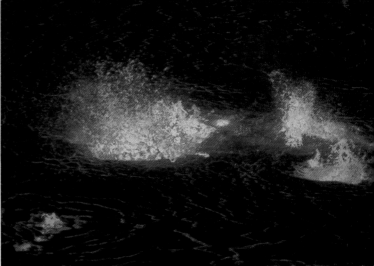

Left: The bleached remains of trees scorched by the eruption of Kilauea Iki in 1959 mark the landscape along Devastation Trail, an appropriately-named path half a mile long. The Kilauea Iki crater is east of the Kilauea Caldera.

Above and below: The dramatic eruptions of Kilauea in 1967, 1971 and 1984 filled the crater of Halemaumau with spewing, pressurized molten lava. The floor of the crater changes its depth with each eruption.

Above: Liliuokalani Gardens Park on the shores of Hilo Bay was named after Hawaii's last monarch, Queen Liliuokalani, who ruled until 1893. This beautiful Japanese garden provides a five acre oasis in the busy city.

Below: The interior of St Benedict's Catholic Church at Honaunau on the Kona Coast presents an unusual blend of art styles. Called the Painted Church, its walls depict Biblical scenes while the ceiling portrays Hawaiian foliage and sky.

Opposite: St Peter's Catholic Church at Kahaluu Bay was built on an ancient temple or *heiau* site.

Opposite top: Plumeria blossoms grow on the tree's forked branches, which bloom continually from spring until winter. The fragrant, long-lasting flowers are favorites for making *leis*.

Opposite middle: The beautiful and dainty Vanda Orchid hybrid is also used for making *leis*. Many are grown for shipment to the mainland.

Opposite bottom: The brilliant Bird of Paradise enlivens many Hawaiian parks.

Left: Dramatic lighting characterizes this spectacular view of the southern end of the Koolau Range, seen from Nu'uanu Pali State Park. The mountains' imposing green and brown walls loom over the fertile coastal plains and small villages nestled at their feet.

Top: Diamond Head serves as a somber backdrop for the brilliance of Waikiki at night. Flood-lit palm trees sway in the cool ocean breeze as the calm water reflects Waikiki's many lights, adding excitement to the night time festivities.

Above: A surfer rests on his board at Sunset Beach on Oahu's north shore. Located between Waialee and Waimea, this is one of Hawaii's most dangerous beaches because of its enormous waves, but it also has the state's finest surfing.

Above: A ranch nestles in a fertile valley at the foot of furrowed mountain slopes in southeast Molokai. Many kinds of flowers and fruits grow wild in the valleys, including bananas, mountain apples, ginger, Java plum and guavas. Forests harbor eucalyptus and pine as well as the native *ohi'a* and ferns.

Below: The afterglow of sunset warms Molokai's north coast. Evenings on the island bring cool breezes.

Right: A gracefully-arching tree frames the mountains of Molokai, including Kamakou — at 4970 feet the highest point on the island.

The beach at Haena Bay on Kauai's north shore separates jagged mountains from crystal-clear water.

Below: The spectacular folds and ridges of Kauai's Waimea Canyon seen from the lookout in this state park are breathtaking to behold. The canyon stretches from the southwest coast north to the Kokee Plateau. The 2857-foot-deep gorge is often called the Grand Canyon of the Pacific.

Right: Wailua River State Park is as rich in history as it is in beauty. On the east coast of Kauai, the park contains the ruins of a temple of refuge, boulders with petroglyphs, royal burial grounds and ancient *heiaus*. The Wailua Falls drop 50 feet to a natural swimming pool.

Picture Credits

Bart Barlow 78bottom, 79top, 81top right & bottom left, 82top and bottom, 86bottom left; Marcello Bertinetti 18bottom left, 19top, 23both, 25top, 64bottom right, 68bottom, 178top right & top left, 179, 368top, 370-1, 372-3; John Calabrese 36-7bottom, 85left, 86top; State of Connecticut 33top, 34top, 37right, 39top left, right & bottom right; Cyr Color Photo Agency: Martin Armstrong (103bottom), Milton Baroody (116-17), James Blank (288bottom, 290-1), Robert Brozek (232-3), Jan Buchar-Artus (94-5), Nancy Butler (136-7), Richard Carkeek (228bottom), James Cigany (323top), Jewel Craig (221bottom right, 226-7, 344bottom), Joe Craighead (231bottom right), William Crocker (169bottom), E J Cyr (92top), Robert Deans (134-5), Michael DelRossi (126top), John Diehl (190-1, 191bottom), Robert Eastburg (102-03), Donald Folland (288top, 289), Dale Friend (334-5), Dan Greenfield (97top, 97-8), Robert Harry (129top), James Jordan (291bottom), Terry J King (113center), Jerg Kroener (320, 344-5), Sheryl McNee (191top, 291top), Charles McNulty (144-5), Randall Medd (126bottom), Claude Newman (127bottom), David Owen (93bottom), Roland Paine (269top), Robert Riemer (150top), Adolph Rohrer (218bottom), Bruce Romick (103top, 104-05, 229, 258, 258-9, 278-9), Daniel Simmons (128top) Fred J Smith (328-9), John Sohlden (186top & bottom), Charlotte Storkamp (162top, 162-3, 166-7), Robert Sweet (230), Tom Swift (96, 97bottom), Larry P Trone (90-1), David Watkins (162bottom), Richard Westlake (116bottom), Harry Williams (151bottom, 216-17), Donald Wright (322); Dartmouth College, Hanover N H 48bottom; Dale Fisher 187bottom; John Foraste, Brown University 28bottom, 28-9; Florida Dept of Commerce, Div of Tourism 146-7, 150bottom, 151top, 152-3, 156; The Freelance Photographers Guild 4-5, 6-7, 10-11, 12-13, 14, 15bottom, 76-7, 77, 100top & bottom, 101, 108, 109top & bottom, 118-19, 120-1, 124, 125top & bottom, 130-1, 148top, 149top, 157, 164-5, 165, 170-1, 172-3, 174-5, 175, 184, 192top & bottom, 193, 212top & bottom, 213bottom, 214, 215top & bottom, 234-5, 236-7, 238top & bottom, 238-9, 260-1, 264-5, 266top, 270-1, 272top, 272-3, 274-5, 276-7, 280-1, 284, 285, 292-3, 294right, 302-03, 316-17, 326-7 332, 333, 338, 340bottom, 357, 364-5, 366, 366-7, 382-3, 384top left, 385right top & bottom, 386-7, 387top, 388-9, 392left 3, 393right 2, 396-7, 399: G Ahrens (49, 89, 115bottom), T Algire (324-5, 354-5), D Bartruff (84, 298top), P Beney (132-3, 139top), N Black (158top middle), J Blank (18bottom right, 19bottom 62-3, 296top right, 297, 299bottom right, 300, 308, 348-9, 353top left), P Boisvert (50top, 52-3), J Bones (262-3), J Brenneis (378,379top), B Byers (49), R Caton (343top), Chicago Stock Finders (80bottom left), W Clay (138), E Cooper (206-07, 352, 362) H Critchell (299top), Cvendler (46-7), F Dole (34bottom, 113bottom), G French (312-13, 351), N Graffman (48top right), F Grehan (354top), P Gridley (78top, 110-11, 296bottom), J Hamel (87bottom), J Harley (361left), Henschel (375bottom), J Hoover (115top), J Hornstein (309bottom right), K Jaeger (309bottom left, 354bottom), A Kearney (342), J M Kordell (298bottom), R Laird (301), T MacCarthy (40bottom right), Marmel Studios (81bottom left, 87top), C McCoy (310-11), McKenney (330top right, 343bottom), Messerschmidt (306-07, 307bottom), S Murphy (304-05), E Nagele (70top, 72-3), Naison Agency (85bottom right), S Osolinski (155, 181, 331top), J Randklev (55top, 106-07, 140-1, 331bottom), Co Rentmeisters (80right, 81top left), Romei (380top left & bottom, 381), G Rowell (360top, 369top), LL Rue II (369middle left), 0 Schatz (360bottom), J Schorr (86bottom right), J Scowen (296top left), L Sieve (295), Sigl (45top), C Smith (51), D Sucsy (88top, 336-7), Tabby (376-7), R Thomas (41, 122top), F G Thoreau (330bottom), A Urba (79bottom right), C Weise (122bottom left), P Weschler (85top right), W Wilson (346-7), G Yechram (309top); Georgia Dept of Industry & Trade, Tourism Div 145top & bottom; Jeff Gnass 1, 20-1, 44-5, 54-5, 68-9, 70bottom, 70-1, 221left & top right, 222bottom, 266-7, 282-3, 286-7, 294left, 318-19, 320, 321bottom, 330top left, 339bottom, 340-1, 341top, 384-5, 389top & bottom, 390-1, 392-3center, 394, 394-5, 398; H Armstrong Roberts 18top, 112, 113top, 241right: H Abernathy (64top right), Avis (40top, 58-9), J Blank (20-1, 21bottom, 32), Burgess (22), E Cooper (254-5), L George (68top), J Irwin (65, 66-7), R Krubner (38), K Krueger (244-5top), W Metzen (240), F Sieb (26-7, 27bottom), J Urwiller (34-5); Indiana Dept of Commerce 197bottom, 198bottom; John and Janine Katsigianis 48top left, 55bottom, 64bottom left, 88bottom left; Louisiana Office of Tourism 166top & bottom; Bill Lurie 368bottom, 375top; Eric Marcusson 79bottom left; Rick McIntyre 222top; Michigan Dept of Commerce 185top & bottom; M A C Miles 61, 116top; Minnesota Office of Tourism, courtesy of Paul Stafford 204top; Montana Travel Promotion 323bottom; National Park Service 148-9; New Hampshire Office of Tourism 40bottom left; New York Convention and Visitors Bureau 74-5; Old Sturbridge Village 15top; Jack Olson 92bottom, 93top, 135top, 160-1, 168, 169top, 182-3, 218top, 220, 223top, 227top & bottom, 228top, 230-1, 231bottom left, 268, 272bottom, 279, 339top, 340top; Rhode Island Dept of Tourism 27top, 31top; South Carolina Dept of Parks, Recreation and Tourism 135bottom; John R Savage 194-5, 196top & bottom, 197top, 198top & bottom, 200top & bottom, 201, 202-03, 204bottom, 205, 210top & bottom, 211top & bottom; Ron Schramm 176-7, 178bottom; Allan Seiden 374top, 379bottom; Sheraton Public Relations Dept 384bottom left; Jerry Sieve 2-3, 42-3, 60-2, 67, 107right, 114, 123, 139bottom, 154, 158top left & bottom, 158-9, 180, 224top left & right, 225, 246bottom, 247, 253top, 256left, 360-1; William Simon 188-9; South Dakota Div of Tourism 213top, 223bottom; William B Stegath 187top right & top left; The Stock Market: J Abraham (250bottom), J Ceshin (252), J Ellenburg (250top), W Hunter (256bottom right), R Morsch (344top) F Parma (253bottom), R Rust (256top), W C Wing (257); The Stockhouse: S Berner (243, 246top, 269bottom), K Carter (245, 251), R Knight (249top), K Krueger (249bottom), J McNee (244bottom), S McNee (241left), T Overlon (248-9), B Senior (242); Douglas Storer 346top, 359bottom right; Strawbery Banke, Portsmouth NH 45bottom; Sugarbush Valley, Warren VT 50bottom; Barry Tenin 28bottom, 30, 31bottom, 33bottom; Tennessee Photo Services 142top & bottom, 143bottom & top left; Tennessee Tourism Development 143top right: Tim Thompson 367bottom left & right, 374bottom, 380right, top & bottom; State of Vermont ADCA 57-8; Virginia Div of Tourisim 127top, 128bottom, 129bottom; Angela White 64top; Wisconsin Div of Tourism Development 219; Wyoming Travel Commission 314-15; Bill Yenne 299bottom left, 307top, 346bottom, 350 353top right & bottom, 358, 359top & bottom left, 363; Zini 88bottom right, 122bottom right.

Acknowledgments

The publisher would like to thank the following people who have helped in the preparation of this book: Thomas and Virginia Aylesworth, John Bowman, Bill Yenne, Joel Zoss, Barbara Paulding Thrasher, and Gillian M Goslinga who contributed to the writing of this book; Jean Chiaramonte Martin and Gillian M Goslinga, who edited it; and Mike Rose, who designed it.